FOUND IT.

D1368154

FOUND IT.

A Field Guide for Mom Entrepreneurs

Jill Salzman

PIGGOTT PRESS
CHICAGO, ILLINOIS

PUBLISHED IN THE UNITED STATES OF AMERICA, SPECIFICALLY IN
FLYOVER COUNTRY
FIRST PUBLISHED AS A PIGGOTT PRESS PAPERBACK IN 2012

The text of this book is composed in Trade Gothic with the display set in Claredon, and the words comprised entirely of letters A through Z.

ISBN: 978-0-9847532-0-8

1. Entrepreneurship 2. Small Business 3. Motherhood
4. Working Moms 5. Chocolate
www.PiggottPress.com

PRINTED IN THE UNITED STATES OF AMERICA

It Takes A Village

I could not be more grateful to these fine folks. Without their help, this book would not be in your hands. One million thanks each to:

Lindsey Obermeier :: Design Goddess, Creens: Design Left of Center
Lisa Guillot :: Book Design Genius, Step Brightly Creative Group
Amy Kalas :: The Incredible Editor, Just Write, Inc.
Jen Howver :: Storytelling Mastermind, VOD Communications
Suze Solari :: Fancy Fashionista, Suze Solari Design
Michele Golden :: Title Champion, Brand New
Jim Mills :: Business Guru, Magnificent Mentor
John Hartzell :: Humor Honcho, Middle Age Riot
Andrew Schulman :: The Super Starter, AMS Consulting
Kathy Katona and Judi Salzman :: Perfect Proofreaders,
The Founding Founding Moms
John Katona :: The Founding Father

to my backbone: Adam

TABLE OF CONTENTS

Introduction

Part 1: Work It

Part 2: Live It

Part 3: Resources

Face It.

Are you a mom unwilling to face the fact that you're an entrepreneur just because you haven't actually started your company yet? Or do you run a startup, but feel it's not a real company because you aren't earning much yet? Are you a brilliant entrepreneur whose stomach turns at the thought of being grouped into the "mom" category? Suck it up. You're an entrepreneurial mama. A mother of invention. A Founding Mom.

If you have even the smallest idea to set in motion—or if you already run a business of any sort—and you've become a parent somewhere along the way, this book is for you. To those of you reading your pregnancy primers AND this book: Kudos! I double dare you.

My first business was a music management boutique, Paperwork Media, established in 2005. I ended up doing a lot more than management by offering artists booking, publicity, and the occasional therapy session, too. With the arrival of my firstborn came the birth of my second business, The Bumble Brand, in 2007. I thought it'd be neat to sell what I called Bumble Bells®, baby anklets with bells on them. Thanks to a fortunate series of events involving Gwen Stefani and People magazine, my little business became what you might call an overnight success. I learned a lot about running a product-based business, and learned fast.

After enough friends with kids asked me how to start their own businesses, I tried on a consulting business and created a Meetup group in my tiny village to bring together a few entrepreneurs that had kids. It was really a selfish act—I wanted to see what their needs were and turn my Meetup members into consulting clients. I expected three, maybe four, women who self-identified as "mom entrepreneurs" to show up. But six months in and 200 members big, I knew that I was onto something. Slowly but surely, what I had dubbed The Founding Moms grew… and grew… and at the time of this writing, we're in 30+ cities with 2,500+ members around the globe.

All of that with no how-to guide? Sounds crazy, right? As you'd imagine, I made a million mistakes. And thousands of Founding Moms later, I've discovered that I wasn't the only one who started my first business by using the 'trial and error method.' A roadmap was missing for the boldest trailblazers on the planet. The collective knowledge of Founding Moms is vast, so I wanted to pack a small but potent amount into a first-of-its-kind how-to guide written just for us. What would I have liked to read at the onset of my first business? Prescriptions and warnings for building and running a startup. And by now, I've gone through enough trials and I've heard about so many tribulations that someone should learn from those experiences. May this book be a baton that I can pass off to you. Once you've got it down pat, please pass it on to the next eager Founding Mom.

Now let's get down to business.

NOTE TO SELVES:

1. No one has, and no one ever will, pay me to endorse particular brands. How would you trust me if I did? If I mention the occasional brand or celebrity and sound like I'm advertising for that person or product, please know that I have not been paid. I really just love them. I'm talking to you, my Pundit Prince, Stephen Colbert.

2. You are most welcome to skip around and read this guide out of order. Mostly during naptimes, pretend-showering or soccer practice. Remember that liquid will ruin the pages, so keep it away from those tiny hands and faulty sippy cups.

3. If your children are grown or super-grown (I'm talking to you, Grandma) this book applies to you as well. We have many, many members of our Founding Moms' Exchanges of the grand kind. As long as you've parented someone along the way, you are a Founding Mom.

PART 1:
Work It.

1 Business Plans: Who Needs Them?

Not you, not me. Trust me. Attempting to gaze into a crystal ball and divine the future does not an entrepreneur make. We mom entrepreneurs are inherent risk-takers. How do I know? Because we jumped headfirst into the chaos and unpredictability that comes with having children, that's how. We played that constant guessing game in our baby's first year of life. Had we planned every single decision of that year, we would have denied ourselves the ability to improvise.

All the texts I read about attachment parenting gave the same advice: Slinging is best for your infant. Don't put your baby down. Soothe with a nurturing touch. Follow the three P's—proximity, protection, and predictability. But all these plans leave no room for improvisation. When she cried, I slung, I swaddled, and I swayed… and when none of that worked on my baby, I improvised. I (dare I say it?) put my baby down and allowed her to spend some time by herself. Did she finally stop crying? Yes. So much for my Perfect Parenting plan.

Had I sat down to write a business plan for my first business, I never would have gotten it up and running. Don't write one. Instead, use that time to actually start working on your business. Jot your thoughts down on sticky notes. Make those to-do lists. Start a daily blog of ideas to keep yourself accountable. Eventually, you can get down to the nitty-gritty and create a bold, detailed business plan, if you must. But for now, while your business is an ever-evolving organism—and like your child, not at all predictable—just dive in. Try it out. Launch that company.

2 Don't Reinvent the Wheel.

Don't do it. Don't start from square one with any aspect of your business. Think you're the last to grasp what "branding" really is? That everyone around you knows how to build the perfect website except for you? That everybody else knows how to use Twitter brilliantly and you're the only one who doesn't get it? Not likely.

Ask around. Be brave. Find the courage to say those words so few are able to utter confidently: "I don't understand." People looooove to give advice. Google searches can help, but you'll get a lot more out of talking to others. Especially in person. After spending five long years building up my own database of music venue contacts around the country, I came to discover multiple websites that populate venue contact information for public display. I've since made a large dent in my forehead from palm-slapping it. I had spent *countless* hours collecting information already available. Don't be naïve like I was. Most of what you want to find already exists out there in some form. Seek and ye shall find.

3 Do the Domain Thing.

Don't wait to buy your domain name. You can hem and haw over the right business name all you want. But snag that domain name right away. Does your new biz revolve around appetizers and is it based in Chicago? Go for AppsChi.com or ChicagoApps.com, even if you decide your company name sounds best as There's An App For That LLC. But get your hands on a domain name right away. Go straight to Namecheap.com or GoDaddy.com. Do not pass go, do not collect $200. Start typing your business name ideas there. The search will help you to narrow down your choices and might spur you to quickly take your pick of the litter. If the .com is not available and you really want a certain name, buy the others—.biz, .org, .info, .us, etc. All of them. In another browser window, conduct a quick search for "GoDaddy (or Namecheap) coupon code" before finalizing your purchase. Add that code at checkout. I'm sure you'll agree that it's pretty darn cheap to buy 3-4 domain names. You'll find this to be a teeny-tiny expense, relative to other expenses that you'll encounter while building your business, and it's arguably the most important.

What's the difference between a domain name and hosting a website? The domain name you purchase can't do anything but give you ownership of that Uniform Resource Locator, or URL, which is simply the address for a web page. You can't build a website with it. You can't use it to interact with your customers. It's like buying a flashlight and trying to use it without the batteries. A domain name is not useful on its own. You need to host the domain name to put it to work. A hosting company will connect your domain name to the World Wide Web. They will give you a plot of virtual land on the Internet. Once your domain name is hosted, you can then build your website, create email addresses, and do a whole host of other things with it.

If you're already running a thriving business with a beautiful dot-com name, you should consider buying sites that mimic or mirror yours but that are off by only a letter or two. Essentially, purchase URLs that include the typos and errors users might type in when trying to get to your site. Like buying FoundingMom.com (no "s") and FoindingMom.com (in case they type an "i" instead of the "u" on their keyboard) when the site is really FoundingMoms.com. Check out http://www.selfseo.com/domain_typo_generator.php. You'll see what I mean. And sometimes it's good to purchase a domain name that stems from your main domain name and concept. If I purchase FoundingMoms.com but people are consistently attending events I call Founding Moms' Exchanges, can you guess what URL I am going to have redirected to my main site? You got it: FoundingMomsExchange.com. And yes, that also can be read as Founding Mom Sex Change, which could actually work out quite well in a different industry if all else fails with my current company.

It's always good to keep your options open.

I've been out of Post-its®
for three months because
I can't figure out a way to
remind myself to buy more.

4 Create Your Game Plan.

Terrified of the word "budget"? Me too.

Don't kid yourself into thinking that you can spend money that you don't have now to make more money later. That helps no one but the credit card companies.

Figuring out what to do with your money can be complicated. When you start a business, there seem to be endless quantities of black holes into which you can throw dollar after dollar. You want to make money. And you can waste lots of hard-earned cash if you don't keep track of where every penny goes.

Figure out a way to keep track of the money coming in and going out. Do it your way. Or even better, do it my way. You won't be able to realistically get a handle on how much you'll have for supplies, staff, yourself, and your next shopping excursion if you have to stick to a useless, hard-to-follow "budget." For the rest of this book and for the rest of your life, refer to your "budget" as your Game Plan. Games are fun, right? Unlike a budget, this sounds like an activity that you can almost enjoy.

Head to FoundingMoms.com/GamePlan to create your Game Plan. Throw a few numbers into any of the worksheets and you'll instantly get a better idea of your spending habits.

When you're able to start winning your own Game by projecting your monetary future, you'll feel totally on top of your Game.

Before consulting a lawyer,

consult a lawyer.

5 Get Legal.

Talking to an attorney for the first time? Free. Getting a second opinion of that first conversation with second attorney? Also free. Checking on said opinions with your accountant? Yep. You guessed it. Free. It's the job of lawyers and accountants to tell you that you should never file anything yourself because you'll miss stuff or mess the stuff up. It's the job of websites like LegalZoom.com to tell that you can "Save time and money on common legal matters!" Everyone has an opinion. You should too. If you are the kind of gal who really digs reassurance and hand-holding (don't be shy—it's better to admit that you do), then pay someone to help make a decision with you (or for you). If you're confident that you can organize your company on your own, or that you can learn how with the guidance of a website, take that route.

What does a bank need from you to open up a business account? It depends on the bank and it depends on your state's rules about business formation. For example, if you are a sole proprietorship, many banks will only need your Social Security number to be able to open an account for you. But if you're doing business under a name that is different from your legal name—even if your name is Jenny Smith and your company name is Jenny Smith Consulting—they may request an Assumed Name Certificate from you. Some will ask for a business license to prove that you're doing business in your state. If you form an LLC or corporation, you may need to show the business tax ID number that you received upon filing and present your Articles of Incorporation to the bank. But, some banks may accept Social Security numbers as placeholders until you get your papers. If you literally stand there before a banker and tell her that you have no clue how to do anything, she'll walk you right through the whole process. Rest assured, most people don't know how any of this works until they've done it.

For my first company, I did everything myself. I filed for an LLC, a statewide (not federal) trademark, and I put an ad in the local papers announcing my existence to the world. For my second company, I

"The first time someone called them **'crayons'** should have been your hint that waxy coloring sticks weren't a new idea."

hired an attorney because I was confident that the second business would be more successful than the first and I wanted to be set up "the proper way"—the way I assumed most professionals do it. Turns out the attorney who was recommended to me not only took three-hundred years to accomplish one small filing, but he messed the whole thing up so much that I ended up paying him legal fees *and* fix-it fees.

Most importantly, lean on an accountant to advise you—the protection that an organized form of business affords you is far outweighed by tax implications that these forms provide. In English, that means that you should not rush off to form an LLC or corporation just because that's what everyone else does and that's what every lawyer advises. Find out what your trusted accountant recommends. It's different for every business. And what should you do after the experts weigh in? Go with your gut.

6 Think Trademarks.

The little ™ that you see next to brand names? That stands for "trademark." It signals that the folks behind the brand filed their application with the United States Patent & Trademark Office (USPTO) to protect it from being taken by someone else. That little ® that you see next to certain brand names? That stands for "registered." The USPTO got the filed application, stamped it a bunch, cashed the accompanying check, and approved the application. Think of ™ as a warning sign and ® as a defiant and firm "don't even try it" message to others who might want to use the same word or term. You want to file for a trademark if you have a genius product or company name that you don't want others to use. You have the option to file locally or to file on the national level for a federal mark, depending on the type of company that you run and it's geographic reach. But, you ask, why file for a trademark, other than to have to figure out how to type that darn little ™ on your keyboard? (It's Option + 2 on a Mac.) Think of it this way: if you come up with a product called Bumble Bells and a person or a company out there sees your cute baby anklets and starts selling their own crappy version and calls those "Bumble Bells" too, you might want to stop them from doing that. They would be taking business away from you and, more importantly, confusing customers about the quality, cost, and reliability of your product (especially if they have a huge publicity machine behind them or a website with tons of traffic). Once you register "Bumble Bells" with the USPTO, that gives you the right to send a 'cease & desist' letter kindly asking that they stop using the product name. If they don't stop and you have a trademark to the product name Bumble Bells, you can sue them. So the real question becomes: if down the line you need to sue an infringer, do you have enough money to actually file suit? If the answer to this question is 'yes', and you would take action against someone in this scenario, consider getting a trademark. If the answer is 'no,' you can still go ahead with your company name and have a thriving and successful business; if another company starts using the same name, you can still sue them since you used the name first but will have slightly less of a solid argument in a court of law without that trademark paperwork. I ran my first company, Paperwork Media, for six years without ever filing for a federal trademark and had no issues, ever.

Filing your own federal trademark is fantastic, but it can be a bit tricky. When I started The Founding Moms, we were "The Momtrepreneur Meetup." Clever name, right? Several months into meeting up, it occurred to me to check out Meetup.com's trademark status. Indeed, the term "Meetup" is trademarked. So, what to do? Change the name. We became "The Momtrepreneur Exchange" and a few months in, I decided to check out the status of "momtrepreneur." It was not, and is not, trademarked. Woo-hoo! I kicked up my heels, created a website, and went whole-hog branding everything everywhere as my organization grew. And this genius that holds a law degree? I went all fancy-pants, wrote a $325 check, and filed for the federal trademark to the term "momtrepreneur" all by myself. I patted myself on the back and went on my merry way, building and building and building some more. Three months after I filed for the trademark, and many Founding Moms' Exchanges in many cities later, I received a big 'ole **DENIED** from the USPTO. Why? Because there are two lovely women who already own the trademark to "mompreneur" and both the word and its meaning are too similar to "momtrepreneur" to grant me a separate trademark. In essence, I'd been infringing on their trademark the entire time that The Momtrepreneur Exchange existed. Fortunately, no lawsuit resulted. Unfortunately, I had wasted a lot of money on design and marketing materials that I could no longer use.

May this story be a lesson to you: if you're serious about your brand and not entirely sure how to do a search, hire an attorney. Several names into my growing organization, I finally got it together to ask an attorney to clear "The Founding Moms" before taking the name. Fortunately, this one stuck.

Bottom line: don't rely on domain names or your own simple searches to signal to you that a certain name does or does not have a registered trademark—I got lucky with Bumble Bells but clearly, no dice twice for me. Hire that attorney when you are ready to make your brand name official. It can potentially save you time and money in the long run.

This is not legal advice.
This is just common sense advice.

*I wish tonight would
last forever.*

I am being audited
in the morning.

7 Account for It.

I've done hundreds of interviews with mom entrepreneurs and have profiled dozens of them on my blog. What's the only business concern that each of these women has in common? Accounting. Whether an entrepreneur tackles company finances on her own or hires an accountant, she usually complains about accounting. While we'd all like to see the money roll in, balancing the books day after day is the last reason that we decide to go into business, isn't it? And at least twice a day my heart saddens and my back aches as I hunch over my computer, click on the Quickbooks icon, and input numbers about which I should care a great deal, but frankly would like to avoid.

If you're just starting your business, I strongly recommend hiring an accountant who can help you set up your books before you go and make a mess of the whole thing. I met my accountant after doing just that: making quite the mess of it all. The accountant's fee was minimal compared to the Everest of paperwork she saved me from by fixing my screw-ups. And what took my accountant a few hours could have easily sucked up an entire day, or even a week, of my time if I had tried to tackle it solo.

If you're one of those abhorrent I-love-math types, check out LessAccounting.com or Freshbooks.com. They come highly recommended and should be easy enough to figure out. There's also InDinero.com, Quicken.com, Peachtree.com, or Mint.com to help you along. Check out these services and see which one fits into your needs. Even when you hire an accountant, it's always recommended to stay on top of your receipts, payments and finances since you're the master of this ship. The Container Store®, OfficeMax®, and Office Depot® offer an array of filing systems for you to try out. I've gone through seven different filing systems and landed on accordion folders, binders, and Excel spreadsheets galore before turning to Quickbooks, and then to LessAccounting.com, and then to an accountant.

If you're brilliant at math or you're an accountant yourself, please forgive the rest of us.

8 Talk Taxes.

DUDE. Make *sure* and doubly sure that you talk to your accountant about all the ways in which your money should be flowing in and out of your bank accounts. Can't afford to hire an accountant yet? Research, research, and then research again your state's tax requirements. Attend networking sessions about it. Go to your local Small Business Association (SBA) office about it. Find a Founding Moms' Exchange in your area and ask questions. A few bad moves on your part could lead to a whopping tax bill, even if you make only a teensy bit of profit. Not fun.

In the first year of selling Bumble Bells, I was not prepared. I didn't think that I would sell very many and I sure as heck wasn't paying close attention to what are apparently "the basics of business taxes" according to the eye-rollers I've since met. (Don't you hate them?) What have I learned since then? Well, did you know that meals are 50% tax deductible if they are conducted for business? I wish I had. And the mileage from your house to a business meeting elsewhere? Deductible. If you use your cell phone solely for business purposes, that's deductible, too. And if your office needs decorating and your office is in your home, the decor is—you guessed it—deductible. The list goes on. Had I been properly educated, or had I even known what to ask, I would have spent a lot less money from my personal account and much more out of my business account. I'd have kept proper track of my business expenses and really paid attention to the fine details. When Bumble Bells started selling like hotcakes, I was slammed with a school bus of a tax bill, and I walked around cursing Uncle Sam for a very, very long time. But really, it was my own fault. Please take the time to understand it and do it right. Once you do, like everything else in entrepreneurship, you will get better at it and the hassle will be well worth your while. Promise.

9 Become a Media Conglomerate.

The *Oxford English Dictionary* defines *conglomerate* as: *n.* A number of different things or parts that are grouped together to form a whole but remain distinct entities.; *v.* To glom together. Since you are now a media conglomerate, it's important that you know what each media category entails. There seems to be quite a bit of overlap and not a lot of explanation. Don't waste a penny hiring someone to help you with "branding" if you don't know what the difference between branding and publicity is.

To help make this whole media thing clear, let's start with some textbook definitions:

Social Media :: from blogs to Facebook to Twitter to LinkedIn to Foursquare, social media refers to a website or mobile technology that permits users to have interactive dialogue. It can be used to assist in branding or publicity for your business.

Branding :: the process of creating and marketing a unique name and image of your company and using that unique name and image consistently as you continue to market it.

Publicity :: the promotion of a business or brand through news stories and mass media to manage the public's perception of that brand or business; usually done by a media outlet or reporter and not the business or brand (so it's usually free).

Advertising :: persuading the public to do something with respect to a business or brand; usually done by the business or brand (so it usually costs money).

Now that we've got that down, let's talk more about how and when to use these tools in the real world of small business.

SOCIAL MEDIA

This can be a wonderful tool for spreading the word about your business and keeping customers up-to-date, but remember: business first, social media second. You can very easily drain a lot of your time by posting status updates on Facebook, remembering to link to new colleagues on LinkedIn, tweeting, tweeting some more, and double-checking all of the resources above for responses and interactions from your many posts. Do it, but don't overdo it. You don't have time to waste. Make Tweetdeck or Hootsuite your friends. They're applications that allow you to manage all of your social media profiles in one place. Master either of these tools and you'll be surprised at how little time is consumed in your workday.

BRANDING

Remember how you toiled over what to name your first child? You wanted to choose a name that either stood for something or that you just loved to pieces. (If you're the long-term-strategy type like me, you also likely chose a name that is easy to say sternly and shout five times in a row.) No matter what name you chose, it had meaning to you. And you put that name everywhere: on the birth certificate and hospital paperwork, on gifted jewelry and kindergarten artwork, on awards and trophies and driver's licenses. Did you change the name along the way? Presumably, no.

The same goes for your brand. Stick with one logo. Stick with one tagline. Don't change up artwork or fliers for different occasions. If you do, how are people going to recognize you? Don't shy away from putting your brand's artwork everywhere, either. If you check out every single page of The Founding Moms' Exchanges, you'll see that each and every single Exchange website has the same logo, the same group name, and the same information. That same logo is even on the cover of this book. If someone asks you for a .jpg of your logo, don't offer up a different logo every time you're asked. Again, how are people going to recognize you if you do that? Same, same, same is our mantra. And while you may grow tired of putting the same stuff everywhere, your brand and business will gain strength, energy, and recognition everywhere. Strong branding works.

PRESS & PUBLICITY

Press. Press, press, press, press. Most clients that I meet are seeking giant piles of newspaper coverage. Press coverage always seems to be the most pressing issue for a business owner, and the most illusory. They want 'in' with online magazines and they want media outlets to review their products or services. I hear it time and time again:

Press will get me soooo far. **Press** will make my business really tick. **Press** will take my company to new heights. **Press** is the only way we're ever going to make bank.

`Stop it. No, it's not.`

If you can get press, that's free advertising that you would have otherwise had to pay for. Congrats to you! But it's not the be-all, end-all that it's made out to be. I once worked with a band whose vocalist quit the symphony. She wanted to pursue her dream of living the rockstar life on tour, and her move made serious waves in the classical music world. Headline-type waves. Cover of *The New York Times*-type waves. After being featured both in print and online at NYTimes.com, the band thought they were golden. Set for life. How many people came to their shows after the coverage? Not many at all. What's the band doing now? There is no band; they broke up. Similarly, after my Bumble Bells were featured in People magazine, we had a good ride. I mean, real good. For eight months. Then, like any other publicity stunt, the oil well dried up and we went back to business-as-usual.

Publicity can take you only so far. At the end of the day, customers and clients will pay for good, quality stuff. And that's that. Pay attention to publicity, but don't make it your Holy Grail. Think of it as company caffeine. It will pep up your business from time to time. But it can also lead to a company crash unless you turn those new customers into a loyal client base.

ADVERTISING

Until you're making money, wait to advertise. Advertising is tempting— particularly when there are online advertising options that seem to cost next to nothing. But who says it's guaranteed to be effective? A 480x480 pixel ad on a mom-focused website only costs $40 and the website says it has 40,000 readers on Alexa.com. Sounds like a good deal, right? But depending on what you're selling, Google Ads may be the way to go instead of that website. It's pretty simple to set up and can be pretty inexpensive depending on your keywords and the amount you choose to spend each day (down to a dollar a day, or even less.) So in a scenario like this, how do you know which is the best place to post your ad? If you don't have a good strategy in place once that ad goes live, the answer is: neither.

I've tried Google ads, the 480x480 pixel ad on mom-focused websites, and a few other avenues of advertising. I had no game plan in place for advertising, and I had no marketing plan to follow-up after those ads ran. So in my case, as inexpensive as it was to do, none of it paid off. Rule of thumb: if you're not sure whether you should advertise, or where you should spend your money advertising, or how you'll follow up once your ad is out there, then you're not ready to advertise.

10 Get Free Publicity.

Thinking of hiring a PR person to promote your brand-new company? Think again. If you're not sure whether you need to hire a PR person, you do not need to hire a PR person. Yet. (Not unlike advertising, when you need to hire a PR person, you will know when it's the right time.) Editors need content for their publications. Bloggers need content for their sites. You can provide them content to promote your business. How? These content providers are very easy to reach.

Here's a little primer to get you started:

1. Get on the internets.

2. In under one hour, you can locate the names and contact information for ten editors of your industry's top magazines.

3. Make a list in Excel, Word, or Tadalist.com. Hit "Save."

4. Write your pitch email. Include a giveaway or discount if you are able to actually give product away or discount a service. These are like bait 'n' tackle for editors.

5. DO NOT mass email it to those ten addresses. Address each email personally, add a customized introductory line that addresses why you are contacting their magazine, then copy and paste your pitch (make sure your fonts match between what you copied and pasted and your personalized additions or they will know that they're not special).

6. Hit send. Ten times.

7. Note in your calendar to follow up in one week, and then a week or two after that.

To-Do List 1:

1. ~~Make list of only 6 items~~
2. Cross off first item.
3.
4.
5.
6.
7.
8.
9.
10.

That's it. Now you're your own publicist.

Congratulations!

Obviously, there will be back-and-forth created with the folks you contact, if they're interested. You may have to get them web-appropriate pictures. You might be asked to ship your product to them ASAP. And you may have to follow up with them even after it's printed—just so you can get yourself a copy of the piece. Once you've engaged 3–5 of these fine folks, you'll have a good grasp on how to continue your efforts. And then you will really understand what PR entails, whether you have the time to do it, and whether it's worth spending some bucks on a professional. It's like making the decision to start a family. When it's the right time, you will know.

11 Blog. Not Too Much. And Mostly Not Using "I."

Follow my logic here: if you're starting a business, you need to market it or no one will know it exists. You will figure out myriad ways to do it, and I know you'll at least cover the basics: website, business cards, the key social media sites (Facebook, Twitter, and LinkedIn). But it behooves your marketing plan to include a blog. Why? Because it allows you to establish a personality for your business. If your website is your virtual storefront, your blog is your real-time newsletter. It offers strangers, customers, and clients a way to read about what's new with you, what's happened in the past, and what's coming up in the future. Think of it as an invitation to see an entire side of your company personality that they cannot otherwise get a feel for by staring at a static website.

When you do get your blog up and running, there are three cardinal rules to follow.

First, do not get so excited that you promise to blog every single day. You will not deliver. That new sparkly thrill about your blog will quickly fade with exhaustion, dinners to cook, and other bits of, oh, you know—running your company. Going from blogging every day to blogging every few days to blogging once a month will cause you to lose readers. You can always blog less and pick up speed if that really becomes your strong suit and/or your moneymaker.

Second, stay away from "I." And "me." And "in my opinion." And "from my experience." It's your blog, isn't it? We know that it's your opinion. Don't be redundant. What's to keep your readers interested in your blog if it doesn't seem tailored to their wants, their needs and their desires and is instead all about you? It only takes one click for a reader to leave and never come back.

Third, learn how to cross-pollinate. You can write yourself silly on that blog that sits on your website and that no one knows to visit. Make sure to introduce yourself to other sites. Swap links. Tweet your blog posts. Link your writings to Facebook so that they show up in your newsfeed once you hit "publish." Get out there like it's your freshman year of college and stick out that blogverbial handshake to meet as many people as you can. By directing traffic to your company, you will boost your e-cred. Post online and watch your business grow like a Chia Pet®.

If blogging is just too much for you, or if you're just not interested, I know that you'll at least send out a monthly newsletter. Right?

12 Stop Using So Many Exclamation Points!!!!!

I'm not kidding!! This punctuation mark is way overused!!!!!

Go back through yesterday's e-mails and Facebook posts. Count the amount of times that you used an exclamation mark. If you can find more than ten of them, you overdid it. We understand that you really do mean what you're saying. And we know that you're a happy person who's emphatic when it comes to…well, just about anything. We send so many e-mails nowadays that by the time you've typed "!" for the fifth time, the recipient of your exuberant email will start to distrust your positive attitude. Every time you hold that shift key down, before you hit that 1, ask yourself: "Do I really mean it?" Actually, make it: **"Do I really mean it?!?!?!!!!!!!?"** If you have to think about it, you don't. Drop those fingers and hit the period key instead.

Here's an example of what could have been a lovely exchange that I ruined with my choice of punctuation:

"Hi, Sara! It was such a pleasure to meet you last week! Do you have time for a phone call today or tomorrow? I'd love to follow-up with you! All the best!"

Don't I sound like a twelve-year old? Now read it without those exclamatory shenanigans.

"Hi, Sara. It was such a pleasure to meet you last week. Do you have time for a phone call today or tomorrow? I'd love to follow up with you." (This was really, really hard for me to write without inserting exclamation points, to be honest.)

When I stopped by _____, there
(name of place)
it was. I knew I had to have it.

The _____ was so perfect. It was _____
(noun)   (adjective)
and _____. My business would run better
(adjective)
because of it. The longer I

_____ it, the _____ I knew I
(verb past tense)   (adverb)
needed it.

So, I reached into my purse to grab my

wallet. But instead, I ended up grabbing

_____, lifted it out of my bag, and
(noun)
everyone there started _____ at what
(verb gerund)
I'd done. The _____ _____ all over me
(noun) (verb past tense)
and then _____ all over
(verb past tense)
the floor.

Why did I have _____
(two-digit number)
kids again?

There it is. Calm, collected, professional. This minor tweak can make a major difference for you and your reader. Head & Shoulders® was totally right. You never get a second chance to make a first impression!!

13 Interact Online.

Don't just Facebook. Or Twitter. Or LinkedIn. Or Foursquare. Or whatever's hot-to-trot right now. Do them all. If you don't know how to do them all—learn. Or hire a young, tech-savvy intern or two. There are some really neat ways to integrate each site with one another. Thanks to an amazing application called Tweetdeck, you can post to Twitter and have it sync with Facebook and LinkedIn. You don't really have to be everywhere—just look like you are. And if you're one of those naysayers who's decided that Tweeting is just not for you, or Facebook is just too time-consuming, or LinkedIn doesn't make any sense for your business purposes, you are wrong. You're building a business, yes? And you want to promote said business, correct? Nothing can get the word out faster and cheaper than social media. Even if you don't understand how these sites are effective, stop resisting. Start asking. Read about it. Ask friends about it. Get on Facebook or Twitter and allow yourself to look silly by posting about how you don't know how to post. Making excuses about why you should not be on there is a waste of time. (Start at Squidoo.com or Mashable.com or E-How.com if you need some how-to tips to get started.)

If you've figured them all out and have your profiles up all nice 'n' neat on the sites and post every few days, and you leave it at that, you're not helping yourself, either. Interactivity is the key. The entire point of social networking is to do exactly that—network online. Just make sure that you interact with several people each day. Introduce yourself and BE BOLD! Or email someone you discover just to tell them how awesome they are. (My most common subject line? "You Are Awesome.") Keep connecting and it will snowball on itself. You will slowly start to see—and reap—the rewards of being proactive.

14 Stop Counting Facebook Friends.

Even better, stop annoying your Facebook fans. It's one thing to interact with potential customers on Facebook. It's another to get sucked into the vortex that is Facebook and kill much more time than is necessary sending thank-you notes, enticing strangers, and creating wall post after wall post of coupon missives and discount enticements. **You could waste weeks trying to lure potential fans to "like" you.**

Your best bet? Converting that energy from working hard on The Big Lure to working toward The Big Steady. The Big Lure is the act of enticing strangers to dig your brand. The Big Steady refers to skipping right past those strangers and instead coddling current customers and clients. By focusing on current devotees, you'll make them feel unique. Special. Loved. And what will your happy customers do? They'll share the love by paying it forward. They'll tell all their friends. That stranger you've been trying to lure with Google Adwords or Facebook ads? That someone might be a cousin or a friend or a third cousin of a friend's friend of a customer. You want that customer to turn to all of her friends and say, "You know what Company X has been doing? It's pretty fantastic. I had the most tremendous experience with them. You should buy from them, too." BOOM! A stranger, converted. And you didn't have to do a thing.

Ever heard of Zappos.com? Maybe you've purchased their shoes or called their customer service about a pair of shoes that you wanted to buy. They're famous for coddling customers by staying on the phone, spending money overnighting orders, sending flowers to customers who have just lost their loved ones—going far beyond that extra mile to make their fans happy. In a similar vein, I used to suggest to the bands that I managed that they send thank-you notes to any and every music fan that bought a CD. That personal touch goes a long way. How long? That fan is usually so excited about being contacted by the band they love that they eagerly share with their friends what happened to them and bring said friends to the

"If you want Martha's Mad Muffins press 1. If you want Martha's Miracle Moisturizer, press 2.

If you are one of Martha's children, stop playing with the answering machine."

next concert—that's two extra tickets sold for the band by someone who essentially conducted free sales on their behalf. All because of a personal touch. To drive the point home: with every purchase of Bumble Bells, I send a personally written thank-you note and throw it in the package. Does it look homemade? Is my handwriting sloppy? Yep. And that's what makes it so perfect. It's personal. They feel the love, and they come back for more.

Pay attention to what matters most. Love the ones who already love you. Build on that. Harness the power of love and you'll build one happy customer base.

15 Don't Answer The Phone.

It's your biggest time suck, isn't it? One phone call distracts you from all that progress. It interrupts your thought process. Here you are, happily working, and one call forces you to stop what you're doing. You reach out, pick up the phone, only to have someone request something of you other than what you were focusing on. The redirect is like a punch to your brain-gut. After addressing the call, you hang up and try to get back to what you were doing. But between the loss of focus from the call and the screaming toddler/whining teenager in the background, it's nearly impossible to get back to your work state.

Now, could that verbal exchange have been accomplished with a quick back-and-forth via e-mail? Probably.

Obviously, not everyone is as tech-addicted as I am, or as I think everyone should be. So it's OK to devote an allotted time each day to the phone. I get that it feels more personal. But since conference calls were created to waste massive quantities of time by encouraging those who love to hear themselves talk to do just that, skip those calls altogether. Creative masters such as Michelangelo, Beethoven, and

"Thanks for you order. Shipping will be delayed until tomorrow because my three-year-old popped all the bubble wrap."

Thomas Edison didn't spend their time stuck in meetings, and neither should you. Instead, ask for a copy of the meeting minutes, or maybe an e-mail of summary points. If your input is truly needed, ask the organizer to e-mail you when they're ready for your input, and get in and out of that call as fast as possible. Then take joy in the fact that you have a whole new pile of hours to use to get things done, on your time and at your pace.

16 Cut to the Chase.

Please do not be vague when it comes to describing what you do. Please, please, please avoid terms like "growth coach" and "consulting expert" and "management specialist" and "business authority."

Why would you pick the broadest of terms to describe what you do? If it's a vague idea that even you cannot explain easily, do better. Imagine if the Millionaire Matchmaker, Patti Stanger, was a "couples expert." Or a "dating consultant." Or even a "love agent." Would you still be watching her TV show? I didn't think so.

17 Kick the Corporate Attitude.

When I started to sell Bumble Bells, I aimed to look as big and corporate and faceless as Kraft Foods. I created a website that didn't allow customers to comment or interact with me. Every e-mail I sent had a signature stating the company name and website without my name. I answered phone calls with a generic, "Bumble Bells, how may I help you?" and eventually outsourced calls to an answering service that did the same. Don't do it. I know it's tempting, but in an era of Internet transparency, this will bite you in the tush.

The moment I became Jill Salzman and not Bumble Bells, my business transformed. Email exchanges became a lot friendlier. Customers who previously sent nasty notes changed their tune. Bloggers started reaching out to review the product. The fear of revealing myself flipped fast and I became the proud purveyor of… me. Old-fashioned customer service turned into a friendly, personal interaction where both sides got a lot more out of the exchange.

The best part? Sales increased dramatically. When I launched The Founding Moms, my goal was to keep the entire company as personal as possible. And to this day, I still do. I'm pretty sure we've grown as fast as we have because I always put myself out there. People connect right away, literally and figuratively.

Be yourself and connect with your clients. You'll be amazed at the transformation that can happen to your company by introducing transparency. It works like a charm.

18 Meet Up.

Human interaction is essential. Nothing compares to the power of face-to-face communication. It's inspiring. It's enabling. It provides a forum for you to gauge a million emotions in one handshake, one nod, and one smile.

What does that have to do with your business? You can only accomplish so much without meeting people face-to-face. Some things need to be done in person. That includes networking, brainstorming, idea sourcing, brand building—you name it. Sure, there's the telephone. And Skype.com. And GoToMeeting.com. And FreeConferenceCalls.com. And UStream.com. And Vokle.com. And FuzeMeeting.com. Hundreds of ways to suck up your time like a Dyson®. But your best bet? Conduct as few online meetings as possible and connect offline instead.

As a first step, I always question whether a meeting is even necessary. When it's a must, I request a coffee over a call each and every time. Why? As a working mother, I don't have time to dilly-dally. Meeting time is time that can otherwise be used to accomplish three times as much. Twenty emails plus two loads of laundry equals one cup of joe with someone else. But if it's true that 90% of human interaction is non-verbal, that face-to-face meeting is essential.

If you find that you're just better at doing business by phone, by all means, get on the phone with folks. But make it as productive as possible. I've managed to whittle down my electronic meetings to one day of calls. I spend two days per week having out-of-office meetings, and that's it. Once a month, I meet with my fellow mom entrepreneurs at The Founding Moms' Exchange: Oak Park and once a month at The Founding Moms' Exchange: Chicago. These Exchanges are such a joy that I spend the following 29 days looking forward to the next ones. And the face-to-face time and human interactions are invaluable.

In reality, you *can* spend five years of your life caring for kids at home while at the same time building up your business through phone calls and e-mails and web research and video conferencing, not to mention talking to yourself. I did.

But with each cup of coffee that I shared across from another person, I found that I engaged with my Starbucks mate in a way that hadn't been, and that can't be, replicated online. I learned that one face-to-face meeting often had the same impact as countless virtual meetings. If a picture is worth a thousand words, a Meetup is worth a million dollars.

19 Network.

Networking does not translate to a Business-Card-Free-For-All or a Make-An-Embarrassment-Of-Drunk-Self-A-Thon.

So, let's set some networking guidelines:

1. Shake hands with whomever you meet at a function.

2. If you strike up a conversation and it feels right to hand out your business card, then (and only then) should you give one up. That said, bring plenty of business cards.

3. If there are nametags, put one on. Which side? Always the right. Think about it: when you stick your hand out to shake someone else's, their eyes naturally follow the arm they're shaking and usually end up on the right side of your body. Location, location, location.

4. Connect with your fellow attendees and find out more about them.

5. Consider offering to speak at a future event.

6. Show up to any and all events where you can contribute. I emphasize the "where you can contribute" part. If there's no connection between you and the group's members, it's not worth your while or theirs. Refine your list to events that can help you, or to those that you can help. Don't head to every event within a 5-mile radius of your house. Do not—I repeat—DO NOT attend 49 events in a row with the same networking group just to have people see your face. I know you're cute, but that face can get annoying.

Stick to this list and your business will blossom.

20 Connect Like an Expert.

Sitting around and waiting for Facebook and LinkedIn and Twitter to "work" for you won't get you very far. Everybody's doing it—and I mean *everybody*.

Most people don't think to take it one step further. Study your contacts both virtual and personal. Their profiles hold a wealth of helpful information. And their networks may include that one person that can help you take your business to the next level.
What do I mean?

Here are some ideas:

1. Go to your high school or college alumni website and search for alums that are now working in your field that may be of help to you. E-mail them.

2. Have a product that needs to be pitched to a major brand or corporation? Search on LinkedIn for all of the employees of that company and see if there are any who are connected to you (or to one of your LinkedIn connections) in your city. Request to connect with them and tell them why you want to connect in two sentences or less.

3. The next time you walk into a place that you frequent—maybe The UPS Store, maybe a local coffee shop—introduce yourself to the locals who work there. Hand them a business card. A friend of mine did this after a friendly chat with a cashier in the checkout line at her local grocery store and got two catering gigs out of it. You never know. I once mentioned to my dentist that I run an organization based on Meetup.com, and it turns out her brother *created* Meetup.com. Small world? Yeah. Is that an advantage for your business? Heck yeah.

4. **The next time someone at the playground talks about something related to what you do, introduce yourself.** I once overheard a guy talking about Twitter before I believed in it. I introduced myself and asked him all sorts of questions. That one conversation turned me into the tweet-a-holic I never thought I'd become. I've also come up with about ten different business ideas just by talking to fellow moms and dads who have idle time while their kids are off playing; the more relaxed, the better to brainstorm.

5. **Invite friends to dinner at your house and demand that they bring a friend that you don't know.** Expand your network and all of their networks into one fun evening.

And that's just the beginning. The world is waiting for you. You just have to think around the traditional ways of connecting and take that extra step.

The people and the opportunities you find will amaze you.

"This seminar is also available on Blu-ray, DVD, digital download, VHS, Beta, Suer 8, 16mm, fotonoveia and View-Master."

21 Add Value.

Doing a giveaway of your product? Give it away with a note that you personally wrote and signed. Discounting your services for a raffle at an event? Add a follow-up call that isn't advertised as part of the package. By adding value to discounted or free products and services, you add heft to your brand. You make it about more than just the product. Make it a personal experience. It's always the simplest, most thoughtful actions that have the longest-lasting impact. It's business, but keep it personal.

> NOTE TO SELF: While you should not be discounting or giving away your products regularly by any means, from time to time you may want to offer a holiday sale or a birthday giveaway. Do it, but do it sparingly, and always add value.

22 Stop Staring at the Competition.

They aren't watching you. Your competition couldn't care less about you. And you'll be sure to drive yourself crazy by constantly staring them down. How is this helping you?

I know, I know. You're just making sure that your specific idea hasn't been done before. If it has, then you'll have to call the whole thing off. And if you already started building your business and your competition is doing this outrageously awesome-looking thing, you now *have* to do it, too—right? Wrong. Re-routing your entire work-week to achieve that new faux-goal is just not worth it. It's really not.

So yes, go ahead and *check out* your competition.

But only for these reasons:

1. You want to research your market and find out who shares space within it; or

2. You want to see who your customers are drawn to, who they're not reacting to, and what programs, incentives, ads, or events are working for your competition; or

3. You want to introduce yourself to your competition so that you can actually work together on building your brands. Who says you have to compete?

If Julie Aigner-Clark had balked at the Playskool® and Hasbro® baby videos that were already out there, would she have succeeded with Baby Einstein®? Likely not. Luckily, she knew her product still had a place in the market. She knew it was different. Likewise, had Reed Hastings stared too long at Blockbuster®, he may never have launched Netflix®. He knew his service was better and he didn't lose sight just because his competition was a giant corporation. Sometimes, variety is just what the market needs. So stop staring *right this minute.*

23 Find a Brainstorming Buddy.

Anne Drew and I are Brainstorming Buddies. That makes us BB's. Do you have one?

We don't call each other to exchange pleasantries, ask about the kids, or muse about why we watch too much reality television. We **THROW DOWN** on the topic of entrepreneurship. We skip the "thoughts about this logo?" or "do you think MyKidsPoop.com is available?" We bring the *big* ideas to the table and really push each other to spread our entrepreneurial wings and fly. Examples of our interactions are akin to, "What are the first five tasks that I must complete to take over the world?" or "If we want to start earning $2.5 million on a monthly basis, how can we implement the right processes to do so?" Even the most minute minutiae are discussed and applied to what we're doing now and what we want to do next. No idea is too big. No scheme is too great. No dream is too crazy.

This BB is your catalyst. As an entrepreneur, you're constantly coming up with a thousand new ideas, and some of us want to implement each of them every single day. As any human being would do, we often second-guess our ideas with "if it hasn't been done, it's probably a stupid idea" or "that just couldn't work—if it could, it would be out on the market already." This is where your BB comes in. There is no judgment or prejudice in the relationship. They're a sounding board for any idea that pops into your head and will give it a fair shake before you move forward with it or shoot it down. You're both mentoring one another and pushing your little cabooses along toward the ever-elusive finish line. You can leave these conversations and say privately to your families, "Man, my BB is CRAZY. Her ideas are over-the-top." But when you talk with each other, the sky's the limit.

"IF I'M SUPPOSED TO FIX YOUR WEBSITE I BROUGHT THE WRONG TOOL BELT."

24 Pay Now or Pay Later.

Go ahead. Google "cheap logo designing services." Seriously, do it. You'll find hundreds of opportunities to have a lousy logo designed just for you. Seek out the most inexpensive web designer and you'll get a top-of-the-line inexpensive-looking website. Pay bottom dollar for product materials and you'll have yourself a basement filled with low-quality products.

A website is a portal to a business' soul. Why hire a mediocre designer to create a "basic" website that you'll have to pay someone else twelve times over to fix, just so you can save a few bucks at the start? That's short-term stupidity. It's frankly not even worth the endeavor to start a business without a contemporary and concrete foundation—your website. In the online world, your visual component counts quite a bit for what you're selling. I hear too many budding entrepreneurs talk about grand ideas, massive distribution, press— and they find the cheapest web designer out there to throw a website together to showcase these grand things. Why, people? Why?

Find out from friends, colleagues, and websites what the proper pricing is for the services you seek. And don't make the mistake of assuming that high prices always mean quality, or that low prices always mean that you're getting great deal. Take the time to review advice from different sources so that you can be as informed as possible before deciding what to invest and where to invest it. My former self did not heed this advice. I've gone through four versions of PaperworkMedia.com and paid five different designers to work on BumbleBells.com, all because I never asked a soul and kept hiring the bottom of the barrel in terms of pricing—and, as I learned, in quality, too. I spoke to a wildly successful CEO three years into my first business who said, "The number one thing I have most definitely learned in fifteen years of running my company is that you really do get what you pay for." Since then, I've gotten smarter, asked around, and have hired the best of the best at a price that I can afford (even though I'd always *like* to spend less.) Now you can even crowdsource for design with sites like Crowdspring.com. Whatever you do, don't

"OK, tell your brother it's time for second shift."

lowball designers. Keep prices more than fair because their work will form your idea's identity in the marketplace. What could be more important than that?

25 Bootstrap It.

Fund your company on your own terms. Do you want control over every aspect of your company? Then scrounge up the money to do it yourself. Think that's not an option and that there is no way to get the money to launch the kind of business that you *really* want? Think again. The allure of venture capitalists and angel investors is a pretty big one—you get a pile of cash in return for giving away a little ownership in your company. Sounds pretty sweet, right? And how about those donations from friends and family? So generous of them. But keep in mind that each of those transactions involving money and people means business relationships, and that would extend this chapter to an entire second book. In short: if you don't want too many hands meddling in your business, find a way to fund it on your own. If there's a will, there's a way to start and run your company without money from other people.

In 2005, when I launched my first company, I didn't know what "bootstrapping" was. Years later I've come to learn that it means launching a company using minimal resources, which is exactly what I did. It took a few hundred dollars to create a decent website for Paperwork Media, and that's all I did. The rest comprised of phone calls, emails, and literally walking around to local shops to ask if they needed help. With each client that I landed, I earned a monthly fee from them and was quickly able to pay back the expense of creating the website. Years later, I got a call from venture capitalists who wanted to buy my company (along with several others) and create a bigger music venture than the one I was running. After an entire year of dealings with trustworthy investors and what seemed like a great deal for me, I bailed. In the short run, that money was very, very, very enticing. But in the long run, the deal would have left me with little control over my own work hours and way less time to spend with my children, so I said no. And my company still survived. No—it thrived.

In 2007, when I launched my second company, I was launching a product, not a service, and thought that it would be impossible to do without the help of other people's money. After much thought, I turned to the people I was doing business with: the importing source of my baby jewelry. They agreed to help my business by waiting longer than usual to invoice me. Because of this arrangement, I had time to build my business and make enough in sales to pay them back on schedule. It was a very sensible arrangement for both parties, and I ended up making more money than I would have otherwise.

If you just can't foresee how to launch by bootstrapping it, you can head to sites like Prosper.com where you can crowdsource loans, or Kickstarter.com where you can crowdsource funding altogether. Family and friends can contribute through sites like these, or they may be able to help you directly.

If you really need to pitch that investor, go ahead and Google local angel investment or venture capitalist firms and ask to speak to the investors directly. But better yet, take a cue from me and work your patootie off so investors come and find you.

Remember the first time your kiddo laced up her boots without your help? You can do it, too.

26 Hire Interns.

Your local high schools and colleges are teeming with students ready to work. Actually, they're desperate to work. They need that sweet spending money to pay for those concert tickets and totally super awesome clothes. Hire them.

Have no money to pay them? No problem. These same students also need class credit, and whether or not their schools will permit the internship, they most definitely need a résumé-builder.

Contact the career centers at your local colleges. Submit a brief job description to the departments that house the kids you're interested in. Reach out to high school principals and inquire about internship programs. Skip the lengthy process of interviewing and get your new interns right down to business. You will be ever so grateful. And when they win Oscars or Grammys or Olympic medals or presidential elections, guess who will be included in their acceptance speeches?

Every summer, I hire a handful of interns who sit around my dining room table and work in various "departments." One student concentrates on publicity; another does website research; and a third, who is getting a degree in graphic design, spends her days creating new logos, posters and fliers. In addition to their services, their fresh perspectives on my business ideas are inspiring. Had I not hired interns, I would still be clueless about the power of Twitter, Facebook, or LinkedIn.

Hire an intern and be the first adult to know anything e-new.

"Mom!

He doesn't
believe you're
out of the office.
Also, I pooped."

27 Hire Virtual Assistants.

Don't have room to incorporate interns into your home office? Hire virtual assistants.

There are a plethora of sites you'll find that offer personal assistants of the virtual kind. You could head over to TasksEveryDay.com, a company based in India and recommended by Thomas Friedman of *The New York Times*. I tried them out and it turned out to be too expensive for my startup needs. The International Virtual Assistants Association has a lovely website at ivaa.org and you're bound to find someone there. You can also look into The Founding Moms' Member Directory where many virtual assistants live.

FancyHands.com is the next best bet to turn to. The site offers an introductory rate of $30 for 15 tasks per month. It's a great way to test out whether or not you're the virtual assistant type. There's Craigslist.org, if you want something more familiar. Or you can try what I now use—oDesk.com. After narrowing my oDesk.com search by type of task (I wanted someone who was a pro at online research), I met Angel. She helped sift through piles of spreadsheets and Internet databases for me, and I was quite happy to have her do so. But I soon realized that I could do the work myself, and I eventually pulled my partnership with Angel to save a bit of dough. It took some trial and error to realize which types of projects are worthwhile for me to hand off and pay someone else to do. For me, delegating graphic design and website projects is a must—I can't draw a stick figure to save my life. Creating spreadsheets, however, is easy for me and is not something that I need to outsource. I also noticed that my 'pay-to-get-this-done' pain point does not surface until I reach a certain limit—that indescribable breaking point where I'm pulling my hair out and I just can't take it anymore. That's when I know to start handing off certain projects to a virtual assistant. And since the ones I hire are in Asia, I've experienced the wonderfully accomplished feeling of handing off an assignment and heading to bed, then waking up in the morning with a completed project sitting in my inbox. If only I could hire virtual daycare.

"DO YOU KNOW A WEB DESIGNER THAT'LL WORK FOR COOKIES?"

28 Barter.

Can't afford to hire staff? Neither can the rest of us.

Bartering is the new spending. Find fellow mom entrepreneurs who need your products or services and trade with them for their products or services. These relationships can be helpful in the short run, and particularly fruitful in the long run if and when the companies with whom you've bartered are as successful as yours. You can take each other to the top. It's happened on many occasions. You can take a peek at U-Exchange.com or NeighborGoods.net to seek bartering partners, but you can also check it out at The Founding Moms' Member Directory which lists, very specifically, mom entrepreneurs with products and services just for you. Do you know the story about the guy who traded a red paperclip for a house? It's true! Talk about some serious bartering skills. (See for yourself at http://bitly.com/jillclip.) Then use his story as your bartering inspiration.

29 Know What You Don't Know.
Really, don't attempt to know everything. Knowing it all is not the point.

The closer you get to "Oh, I get how to run a business!" the more in danger you are of becoming outdated, behind the times, done, finished. You can't ever conceivably know everything. You should not even try to know it all. Admitting that you'll never know everything will help you overcome your fear of "I have no idea what I'm getting myself into." I'm many years in and every day continues to be one giant learning curve. With each new issue that arises, I figure out yet another new way to do things. Or a new website to read. Or a new Founding Mom to profile. It really never ends. Sometimes I figure it out on my own, and sometimes I figure it out with some help. The day I get close to knowing it all is the day I will fire myself.

"LET US
HANDLE
ACCOUNTS
RECEIVABLE.
We could play good
cop/stuffed cop."

30 Fake It.

It's ok to have no idea what you're doing. At the beginning, I didn't either. When you get together with friends and family, fellow entrepreneurs at Founding Moms' Exchanges, or other safe havens, talk about what you don't know. Ask questions. Don't be afraid to look stupid—because you won't.

But when you're putting yourself out there in the market to customers, clients and companies who can help/partner/share/buy/hire/work with you, fake it 'til you make it. The more confident that you sound to them, the more confident you'll feel about what you're selling. And the more times you repeat your confident pitch, the more you'll believe it. Fake it enough times and you'll actually make it.

During my internship at Zagat Survey, restaurant guide guru Tim Zagat was kind enough to take the summer minions out to lunch. We went to a very fancy restaurant in Manhattan as a "thank you" for our hard, unpaid work. At that time, the Internet was a brand new invention and the restaurant review powerhouse had just thrown together a bare-bones website. Over fine wine and Lobster Newburg, Mr. Zagat asked what we thought of the website. He went around the table and one by one, he got "Looks great!" "You're really onto something!" and "Bravo, pass the wine!" I was last—and I was clearly a bit more comfortable lying than the rest of them. "I know exactly what you need to do to lure more viewers to your site." I made up several suggestions on the spot, using the salt shaker and the butter knife that I was holding as visual aides. After that lunch and for the rest of the summer, I became his go-to gal for redesigning the website. And while I can't take any credit for the company's current site at Zagat.com, two decades ago I advised on the fly—and because I sounded confident, the head of the company trusted me. (Sorry, Tim!)

Go ahead. Make stuff up. Someone will believe you.

31 Finish What You Start.

Starting up your own company is awesome. **I'll say it again: starting up your own company is awesome.** Thinking up a name. Creating a logo. Telling your networking group how great it's going to be. Getting that first client. It's all so exciting.

Sustaining it is not.

The Intro Glow will eventually wear off, and then where does that leave you? There are countless blogs sitting on the Web with old content. They haven't been updated in years. There are countless basements filled with product prototypes collecting dust. Don't let your great idea end up a dustball. Start everything you do for your business with an I'm-in-it-to-win-it 'tude and then convince yourself that you'll never quit anything. Then don't quit anything.

Launching a whole company is not for the faint of heart. Think long and hard not only about how you are going to kick off your idea, but about what you're going to do after it's smoothly up-and-running. How will you maintain your business? And more importantly, what will you do to keep spirits high and carry on that verve and energy that you had when you launched? That's the kicker. That's the part that most entrepreneurs don't think about—because the start is our favorite part. That's why we got into this. Many of us are start-up junkies. If you know you really only like to start things, find an operations manager or partner to hand it off to once you've launched. Since we're talking startup here and you likely won't have the funds to pay someone to take over, make sure to ask these questions of yourself at the get-go. Remind yourself that you want to be a massive success— and that success comes not with a launch, but with follow-through.

You have no choice but to finish what you started when it comes to raising a child. Make it the same for your business. Finish what you start.

32 Get Down to Business.

Here's the order in which I always start up a company.
I suggest you do the same.

1. **Enter domain name ideas into Namecheap.com or GoDaddy.com while thinking about company or product names.** If you come up with the perfect company or product name without checking either site, you'll be at a major loss from the start. Let's pretend you want to call your company, "Workaholic." If someone already owns Workaholic.com, you'll likely end up choosing something like WorkaholicSite.com or WorkaholicOnline.com, neither of which any customer or client is likely to remember. Best to start your branding right, right from the start.

2. **Once you've purchased your domain name, you'll need to host that domain somewhere.** GoDaddy.com can host your domain name or you can find a smaller company that can answer your questions quickly without a generic support hotline. I use Phillips Data and have been happy with them every day for seven years.

3. **Pick out ten websites that really appeal to you.** Compile these into an e-mail message or a Tadalist and save that to refer to later. Then shoot an e-mail query to the designers of each of those favorite websites. Ask how much it costs for a basic website, and do some price shopping.

I need to pause here.

This pick-your-designer bit is like choosing a place to live. You really need to get to know the type of place that you will inhabit before making it your home. If your gut tells you that the few websites you've seen of their work are just not cutting it (even if it's only the colors that you dislike), don't bother. You should hear yourself squeal in delight when you look at their previous work. That's how you know you're onto the right designer. Find beautiful work first, then

Let's start a to-do list of things we've already done so we can cross them out.

To-Do List 1:

1. Start a To-Do list.

compare pricing. This designer will not only help you to introduce your e-persona to the world but he or she will hopefully be tweaking your site along the way as your company grows and flourishes. You want a strong relationship with them. I've gone through about 4,823 web designers at this point in my career, and my first impression or gut instinct has been right each of those times. (Although, clearly, I've only listened to it one time.) And upon finding my favorite designer in the whole world some time ago, I haven't looked elsewhere since. I repeat: you always, always, always get what you pay for. None of that template crap is necessary, and if you really can't afford to work with a solid graphic designer, then wait on designing a website altogether and start with a free site at Tumblr.com.

4. **Head to your local UPS Store and rent a box.** They'll give you, say, Box #123. When printing your business cards or filling out forms, you can call it Suite 123 or No. 123. It will still reach you. It doesn't cost much to have privacy and to separate your business from your home address, which makes Uncle Sam happier, too—particularly if you're running a service-based business. I don't have enough fingers to count the number of times that a wannabe-client has stopped by my "office" to play me a tune or sing or dance or rap to me and has then so brilliantly followed up with an e-mail that reads, "Dear Jill, I tried to stop by your office today but could only find The UPS Store in its place. Can you direct me to your office so I can play you my new, hit song for you? Peace, DJ Killaz."

5. **Figure out how you want to file your business, legally.** Once you know whether you'll be a sole proprietorship, an S-corp, an LLC, a C-corp or a partnership, file away. Make sure to apply for a Federal Employment Identification Number (FEIN) at www.bit.ly/feinapp. It's free and will take you about three minutes to get one.

6. **Open a bank account.** If you're not a sole proprietorship, take your Articles of Incorporation with you, too. Ask around to see which businesspeople are using which local bank, which offers the best rates, which is the most welcoming to mom entrepreneurs, and so on. Then walk through the door and announce loudly that you NEED A CHECKING ACCOUNT FOR YOUR NEW BUSINESS, and get that business bank account opened.

7. **Consider registering for a trademark or a service mark.** If you're creating a product that has the cutest name ever, or you've just formed a band that is heading out on tour, you may be interested in registering a trademark for your name (or in some instances, filing for a service mark and not a trademark.) There's plenty to read about this at http://uspto.gov, and you can find those forms to fill out and file there, too. If this isn't something you intend to do or want to do right away, don't. It's optional. Just keep it in the back of your busy mind to consider as your business grows.

8. **Hire a great graphic and/or web designer for logos and branding.** This designer can help you with all of your branding needs—from logos to letterhead to business cards, and more. Not unlike the advice above about finding a graphic designer, do the same to find yourself a website designer. Your graphic designer may indeed be a website designer, too, but more often than not they are separate pieces of the pie. (If you *can* find someone who can do it all for you, hooray!) Remember, your website will be the face of your company for years to come, so choose carefully.

9. **Set up your social networking sites.** Facebook? Check. Twitter? Check. LinkedIn? Check. Then connect with me at Facebook.com/foundingmoms, Linkedin.com/in/foundingmom and @foundingmom. Then connect to everyone else you know and tell them all about your business. Go to Knowem.com to find out the other sites you should join, too.

10. **Get to work.**

PART 2:
Live it.

33 Define Yourself.

Say that you *are* it. Not that you're *going* to be it. Not "I'm opening up a new restaurant soon." But "I am a restaurateur whose grand opening for my new joint is happening next month." Not "I'm thinking about starting a pet training company." But "I am The Dog Whisperer." Not "I'll be starting to sell my jewelry on eBay soon." But "I'm a jewelry designer." Golda Meir was right: "Don't be so humble; you're not that great." In fact, you appear even less great by shying away from what perception you want people to have. Perception is everything in business. Start out strong. Even if you haven't started yet.

We can also be very evasive since motherhood is an excellent excuse. "I'll get this started when Chuck is in preschool," or "I'll start charging clients once my kids graduate." I get that you're busy. But from a business perspective, why wait? Try it out even if it never ends up happening. You might just like the sound of it so much that it actually *will* happen.

You can also be picky about what you put online. Those websites that prompt you to fill out a complete profile? Be careful. If you keep clicking away on a site like LinkedIn or About.me, you'll soon be adding all sorts of things to your profile to fill up space and look uber-important, like your award for perfect attendance junior year of high school, or that bartending job you had over twelve years ago. Think hard about the information that you include. Not all of it is necessary. What do you really want your peers and clients to know about you?

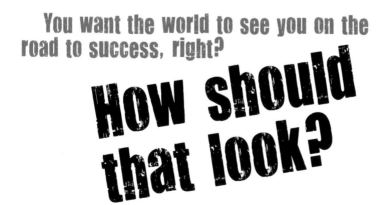

You want the world to see you on the road to success, right? How should that look?

"You should
do what
you love

and i love
hugging
bunnies."

34 Don't Sweat It.

Park your children at the TV while you work. Offended by my suggestion? Then try a new approach—hire them. Make them your tiny assistants. They can color, draw, stack, stuff, stamp—miscellaneous duties that can actually help you. Yes, they will scream into the phone. Yes, they will rearrange all of the papers on your desk so that only they will know where to find anything. Yes, the entire document that you just typed out will be deleted because IF YOU DON'T GET OFF MY CHAIR RIGHT NOW I'M GOING TO GIVE YOU A TIME OUT.

Such is your life. It's the fighting it that really stresses us out. "Real" entrepreneurs don't have to deal with these irritations, interruptions, and WHY ARE YOU PEEING IN THE DOORWAY WHEN I TOLD YOU TO GO TO THE POTTY? It's a touch of the "Why me?" syndrome. Don't go there. Instead, post a calendar on your wall titled Countdown To Preschool and welcome them into the workforce. I'd be a millionaire if I had a nickel for every time that I was literally dying from fear that my kids would have a meltdown while I was on a conference call. And then it happens…over and over again. The screaming begins. I mute the phone to yell BE QUIET! And then I forget to mute the phone before I yell again. And all the call attendees start chiming in with things like, "Is that a cute little nugget I hear in the background?" or "I just had my first!" We all laugh it off and get back to business. When this happens to you, good chance you'll be pleasantly surprised, too. Don't sweat it.

35 Practice.

In his book *Outliers*, author and brilliant thinker Malcolm Gladwell introduced to me the "10,000-hour rule" which is based upon the theory that if you practice a specific task for 10,000 hours (or, on average, 10 years)—you'll have success in it. So following this train of thought, geniuses like Mozart or The Beatles are not really overnight successes—rather, they honed their art for over 10 years and became quite good at what they did. This theory can apply to anything. Chess masters, movie stars, physicians, and mechanics can all

" Will you still take me to ballet class now that you're incorporated? "

become brilliant successes with practice. And guess what? It applies to you, too.

Want to become the biggest, best, and brightest star in your field? Stop skipping the seemingly simple stuff and practice every bit of your business. Learn all of the ins and outs. Take your time. You can't rush the hours any faster than they're already going. And take solace in the fact that you'll be *great* in no less than 10 years. (And that doesn't mean you can't make money in those 10,000 hours. You can do that, too).

36 You Do Have Time.

I know, it never feels like you do. How can you pack in feeding your family, driving children all over town, answering e-mails, checking your smartphone, scheduling doctor appointments, participating in conference calls, changing diapers, helping with homework, and feeding the dog without losing your mind?

Make a list. Keep it to five items in length and only encompass work to-do's. Spot areas in your day when you can accomplish each of those five items. When you're done at the end of the day, check off what you can, and then cut the panicking short if it's not all done. You don't need to do everything all in one day. Remember Rome?

Slowly build systems for yourself that work for *you*. Maybe you like to cook all weekend and make family meals so that you can focus on work all week. Maybe you think most clearly in the evenings and working in the mornings isn't really cutting it. Maybe your dishes or laundry tasks aren't working for you and you hand them to your partner, to your kids, or to Saturday. You lead an alternative lifestyle now, and part of the success in living it comfortably is facing that fact. Experiment. Find the schedule that suits you.

Walk around with a pen and paper at all times. Put a recording device in your purse. If the BlackBerry's not doing it for you, purchase a cheap laptop to take everywhere. (Excuse to buy an iPad, anyone?) Invest in a Bluetooth device so that you can make calls without crashing the car. Spend an hour working at the library instead of your home office. Plan out your week on the weekend prior, or plan out your day the night before. Shut down technology that can interrupt you during blocks of quiet work time. Download programs like Sticky Notes or Things or Doomi or Tadalist.com (my fave!) and compile lists of to-do's that are not urgent. Flexible hours are a mindset. Throw out the nine-to-five tradition and make your schedule work for your life.

Stick an hour in between all of the above to relax. Rest. Unwind. Read. Exercise. Yes, you do deserve it. And remember to stop giving yourself a hard time for what's not been done. Focus on what has been done and be proud of yourself. I am proud of you.

37 Get Feedback.

Ask for it. Beg for it. We live in an interactive world filled with social media and social events. There's never been an easier time to get feedback from friends, family, clients—even strangers. And with feedback, you can keep a pulse on the market, on your company, and on your product or service.

If you think that you should avoid getting your business ideas out there because you're afraid someone will steal them, think again. It takes a lot of hard work to steal an idea and put it into motion. And that customer feedback is way too valuable to miss out on just because you're worried that there could be an infringer out there (who likely won't know how to build a company based on your idea anyway.) Feedback is what allows you to make your product or service the best that it can be and to keep your client base happy.

If you want to stay mum and skip the customer feedback because it's too hard to figure out who and how to ask, you're shooting yourself in the foot. Figure it out. If you were able to figure out all of the ins and outs of starting your company, you sure as heck can find a way to tap into a crowd who would be interested enough in your product or service to provide feedback.

There are plenty of ways to go about it:

1. **Google it ::** Locate Meetups or events where like-minded customers and clients are hanging out

2. **Post queries in online forums, on blogs, and on Craigslist**

3. **Email bloggers, family, or friends**

4. **Host focus groups with prizes to entice folks to offer feedback**

5. **Post a survey on Wufoo.com or SurveyMonkey.com and tweet it out to your followers**

Feedback is priceless. You can't put a price tag on the profits it can bring you. Once you discover how easy it is to ask for it, you'll be kicking yourself for not bugging folks for feedback long ago. You can finally stop guessing what your customers want or need. It's so much easier to just let them tell you.

38 Got Guilt?

How much do you love that there's even a website about this? WorkingMomsAgainstGuilt.com is a brilliant site, forum, and kvetch chat room where it's reinforced time and time again that we must work without guilt. I do want to make one thing clear, though: you will feel guilty. We all do. That's the core of the work-plus-kids dance that we dance. You can fight it, give in, and feel horrible about yourself, or you can keep biting your fingernails as you listen to the stay-at-home moms in the park talk smack about working moms and how much they ignore their kids. The secret? Your kids only know their world. And if their world includes Mom at the computer more frequently than their friend Delilah's mom, it's OK. They're not living in Delilah's world, now, are they? The comparison to other kids' mothers is akin to staring at your competition while trying to build your business. It only feeds your guilt and negativity.

You are an example of empowerment to your children. You're showing them that they, too, can have a strong work ethic. If you're focused on your iPhone or spend an hour at the computer while they do their homework, it's not a sin but a blessing. And mostly, it's just your childrens' way of life. Going over all of the associated pessimistic views—self-centered, absorbed, negligent—won't do you any good. My little girls definitely say things like, "Time to finish e-mailing, Mom," and "Are you going to go work now?" Do I feel badly? Some days. Do I stare at their little faces when they say those things and realize that it's not out of self-pity that they say it but it is simply an expression of their own actual lives that they're living (which just so happen to include mommy working)? More often than not, I do. They know no other life. My favorite moments that reinforce how normal working mommies can be are on Saturday afternoons when my toddler plays with her friends and I overhear her asking her guests to sit behind her in her toy car so that they can play "Let's Go To The UPS Store®." Priceless.

39 Sleep.
Basic needs, people. Basic needs.

A former mentor of mine, Mary Carskadon, Ph.D., studies sleep at Brown University. She says, "We just ignore these bad feelings from not enough sleep and get used to it. We forget what it's like to feel good, and how much more efficiently we can do things." Although there are thousands of theories out there about what a good sleep schedule looks like, on one thing we can all agree: you need sleep in order to function. The more tired you are, the less you can retain. You can't keep anything organized, and forget about returning phone calls. Puhleeze.

Popping Advil and downing coffee isn't the best path to a lucid thought process. A neat rule of thumb I adhere to is this: sleep. If getting a delicious eight hours trumps re-runs of *The Cosby Show*, I will suffer the consequences. And every night that I indulge in reading a book for an extra hour when I should be sleeping, I kick myself in the shins the next morning and go through my day waiting for bedtime to roll around again.

Stop the madness. Go to sleep. You'll be a changed woman. You'll have energy to share with your family. And your company will thrive. (Note to new moms: change the word "sleep" throughout this chapter to "nap.")

40 Find Balance.

I was pregnant with my first daughter and very, very scared to tell my clients about it. By the time I mustered up the courage to ask them for two weeks off, the fear was moot: I was showing and couldn't do anything about it. That was my first mistake.

When my firstborn was just six months old, sitting up and soon to be crawling, I became very, very scared that her daylong naps were coming to an end. What did this mean for my business? There could be an infant's howl intruding on each and every call that I would make. I might start to be late for meetings since she was getting

"That's not a new perfume. Lizzie and I spent all day making an origami zoo out of used fabric softener sheets."

clingy. What did I choose to do? Go the very expensive route of park-ing her in daycare. *All because I feared ruining my business.* You might say that I put business before children. I did.

Years later, I chuckle at the fear that child rearing can bring into an entrepreneurial woman's life. There was no one who was able to tell me, "It's OK in today's workplace to have a kid interrupt a busi-ness phone call." There was no one around me who had endeav-ored to do her own thing in her own home with her own kids. But I've found that every customer and client who *has* kids actually feels warmer towards me for putting it out there. Those who don't have kids yet find that it makes me more personable, more real, more accessible. Accessibility might not have been such a hot commodity once upon a time. But times have changed. Rest assured, you can now spend time working on building your company and minding your children. Seek the balance that works for you. Work with your kids, not around them.

41 Get Organized.

It is rare that a mom entrepreneur shares what her home office is like. Even if you work in a shared office space from time to time, you've likely carved out a space in your home to get work done. Some home offices are straight out of a Pottery Barn catalog. Others? Not so much.

Having lived in three different homes throughout each of my start-ups, and being the list maker that I am, I've compiled my go-to list of stuff that I need in my workspace.

You may need none of this, but if you need an excuse to go on a shopping spree, here you are:

1. **A desk.** I once used the top of a washing machine. Then I upgraded to Ikea's Fredrik standing desk. With each pregnancy I've had to sit back down; the 4' x 2' workspace suits me just fine.

2. **The largest pencil holder in the world.** I prefer pencils to pens, specifically the gigantic My First Ticonderoga No. 2 pencils. Loads of pens and pencils fill it up along with one ruler and at least 3 pair of Fiskar scissors. You just never know.

3. **One hundred million trillion sticky note pads.**

4. **Two calculators.**

5. **One printer/scanner.** My HP Photosmart All-In-One has lasted for years.

6. **NeatDesk Scanner.** Expensive and awesome.

7. **Garbage pail for snack wrappers, more snack wrappers, and my children's bad art.** (No such thing, I know.) Separate wastebasket for paper to be recycled.

8. **A shredder.**

9. Inspirational photos. And by inspirational, I mean hysterical. And by hysterical, I mean Carol Burnett wearing a giant feather headdress.

10. One stapler, one pile of paper clips, a handful of binder clips, one rubber band ball, and one tape dispenser. My toddler is very familiar with this set-up as well—we know a kid named Spencer whom she only refers to as Dispenser.

11. Lined pads, note pads, and any and all forms of paper stacked on one shelf with 3 variations of envelopes. One is the manila folder type of envelope with the clasp at 8.5x11, one is a business-sized white envelope for regular mail, and one is a manila business-sized envelope to hide those checks that I mail.

12. I hang my rolls of return address labels on fishing wire strung between two walls. This system makes for easy rolling and sticking.

13. Glasses, lip gloss and gum for impromptu Skype calls. I know you can't smell my breath over the Internet yet, but I am prepared for when that day comes.

14. IdeaPaint on one wall. It turns your wall into a giant whiteboard.

15. On two standing shelves across the wall from my desk, I have my files, bills, wrapping paper, padded envelopes, juice boxes, ribbon, *Goodnight Moon*, puzzles, a piggy bank, CDs, and a map of the world. Professional organizers would become violently ill in my workspace, but it works for me.

" Very good, dear. Now let's take another crack at that label maker. **"**

I had a rough day
with the kids
but I think I
finally got the
magic marker
off my ass.

41 Manage Your Time.

Even the most seasoned entrepreneur has been known to struggle with the art of time management. And you are no exception. So how should you manage your time? It's one of the most common questions asked by mom entrepreneurs when it comes to running their businesses. But there is no one right answer. Everyone's process is different.

That said, instead of sharing the ways that I manage my own time, I thought it would be beneficial for us all to learn some tricks of the trade from a pile of Founding Moms. Take a look at how they practice time management. And don't forget: there's no one particular way to manage your time. Just the way that works for *you*.

SCHEDULE IT

"I recommend using an online calendar to keep up with daily appointments. On the weekends, use Saturday and Sunday for catching up on paperwork and preparation for the next week."
La'Shon Anthony, visuals4u
Visuals4u.com

"Use only one calendar that you can update and sync between your laptop and your mobile or tablet, and one that can be viewed whether you're online or offline."
MJ Tam, Chicagonista and Social RevUp
Chicagonista.com and SocialRevUp.com

"Complete a detailed weekly schedule of when you will work and stick to it. Use the schedule to be focused on necessary tasks throughout the week and then focus on your family outside of your work hours."
Jenny Untermeyer, TravelKiddy
TravelKiddy.com

TIME TO-DO 1. 2. 3. 4. 5. 6. 7. 8.

"Instead of adding everything you need to accomplish to a 'to-do list,' pick only your most important tasks (which honor your priorities), and schedule them in your calendar like you would a doctor's appointment or a client meeting. For example: Tuesday, November 3rd, 10-11 a.m: Complete proposal for Client X and email it. By choosing to carve time out of your day to accomplish your priorities, you'll feel better about getting the most important things done."

Lara Galloway
MomBizCoach.com and MomBizRetreat.com

LIST IT

"Set goals. Plan and schedule everything, even your personal and family time. Small business owners have multiple tasks to complete daily. If you don't plan and schedule you may forget something important!"

Beverly Cassidy, Beverly Cassidy Photography
BeverlyCassidyGoingPro.com

"I find it helpful to make lists: current/immediate tasks, this month's goals, and long-term projects. A monthly calendar in my purse helps me to plan ahead long-term, and my mobile device calendar helps me to keep track of daily deadlines. Multiple lists and calendars allow me to make use of even a few spare moments of time because they allow me to focus in on specific unfinished tasks at a moment's glance."

Audra Adomenas, Just For Trees, Inc.
JustForTrees.com

"Three a day keeps the worries away! To feel accomplished while not burning out, I schedule three tasks a day. Work tasks make the list if they lead to actual sales. Personal tasks must clear up time for play! Once complete, I get the luxury of picking up other items while knowing the good stuff is getting done."

Dina Eisenberg, Hassle Free Contract System
HassleFreeContracts.com

"Either be an anal list-maker like me or plunge into darkness and confusion. Set aside specific 'appointments' with yourself and stick to them!"
Adrianne Stone, Writer and Certified Health Coach

"When planning your days, glancing down a to-do list can be misleading because a single entry that takes one line to write could take two minutes (a phone call) or two hours (a proposal). Therefore, when you add an item to your to-do list, it's important to include an estimate of how much time to allow for that task."
Elaine Quinn, Author and Professional Organizer
NoPlaceLikeWorkingFromHome.com

"Don't overload your daily to-do list! Only put things on your daily list that *must* get done so that you can really focus on what's most important and at the end of the day feel like you have used your time wisely."
Alicia Peiffer, Living Your Moment
LivingYourMoment.com

"Group your to-do list based on what kind of task it is: CALL, DO, ONLINE, etc. Then do as many of them at the same time instead of toggling between different kinds of tasks."
Kat Gordon, Maternal Instinct
MaternalInstinct.com

"Have a maximum of two things on your to-do list on any day, and make sure you get them done! Also, keep a schedule with the kids (dinner, bath, sleep etc). Without this you won't accomplish anything!"
Nivi Raghunath, Rani's Adventures
RanisAdventures.com

DONE 1. 2. 3. 4. 5. 6. 7. 8. 9. 10. 11. 12

"My to-do list for the next day always includes some easy, quick-hit tasks that I can knock out in that first hour of work while sipping my morning coffee. Accomplishing so much at the start of the day and getting the 'rush' that comes from crossing off those to-do items lightens my mental workload and inspires me to get through some of the more time-consuming tasks on that list."

Amy Kalas, Just Write! Inc.

PLAN AHEAD

"Mom entrepreneurs often work irregular schedules, squeezing in work sessions whenever they can. To take advantage of every minute, at the end of each work session, take five minutes to determine what you will do during your next session. This way, when you next sit down to work you will not waste any time catching up."

Sarah Giller Nelson

LessIsMoreOrganizers.com

USE AN APP FOR THAT

"Zite is an app that creates a customized reading experience on my iPad2. All the subjects I'm interested in reading about show up in a very tidy platform."

Jacqueline Smith, Kiesque, Inc.

Kiesque.com

"With so many websites and so little time, I used to miss a lot of great articles and activities…until I found Instapaper. It's a free app to save web pages for reading later. When you find something you want to read, you just click Read Later. Then you can come back when you do have time, or read your articles on the go."

Maggie Welles, Artist Enterprises

Time To-Do 24. 25. 26. 27. 28. 29

UNSUBSCRIBE

"I save all the email newsletters I receive in a separate file. Then, once a day I go through them. If I find that there is a newsletter that I'm frequently deleting or ignoring, I unsubscribe to reduce email clutter. By clustering the time spent reading them, it a) makes it more obvious how much time I actually spend on electronic 'junk mail' and b) saves me from distraction as they're coming in throughout the day."

Kelley C. Long, KCL Financial Coaching

KCLMoneyCoach.com

JUST DO IT

"Prioritize: What task or activity has the most serious consequence if you don't do it? Do that first. Not everything has to be done at the same moment. Don't let your OCD get in the way. Delegate."

Adrian Miller, Adrian Miller Sales Training

AdrianMiller.com

"The best tip I ever received was to touch something only once. You receive a bill, pay it right then; getting changed, put the article of clothing where it belongs right then. It takes twice as much energy to put something in the wrong place (as in not putting it away) as it does to just put it away, in the right place, immediately."

Maura Braun

MyDesignerOnline.com

"Procrastination is not an option. If you have limited time to accomplish tasks, make lists. Then do each task in stages, so you can make progress daily in small steps."

Suze Solari, Suze Solari Design

SuzeSolariDesign.com

30. 31. 32. 33. 34. 35. 36

"Just do something. That's what I tell myself when I feel over-whelmed by a pile of divergent tasks, especially ones that require multiple steps and can't be easily checked off a list with one swoop. Rather than succumbing to procrastination, I set a reachable goal of simply doing one step of one item on my list. Once I get moving, I generally end up tackling more than that, but the low expectation is enough to get me started."
Erica F. Smith, Erica Gail Inc.
EricaGail.com

TO MULTITASK OR NOT TO MULTITASK?

"Working from home, I need to manage the household and my time, so I follow the ABC's: Always Be Carrying something. Answering the door? Pick up toys and shuffle shoes to the side as you go. Carrying the baby upstairs? Grab your sweater and purse to put away for the night. Founding Moms take multi-tasking to the next level."
Lisa Guillot, Step Brightly Creative Group
StepBrightly.com

"Avoid multitasking whenever possible. I find that trying to get work done while caring for my daughter is usually very frustrating for both of us."
Jessica Pfohl, Unearthed Paints
UnearthedPaints.com

"If you work from home, when making breakfast for your family, make lunch and snacks for the day at same time. Then you only need to prepare food once and will have less cleaning up the kitchen during the day."
Melissa Luhrman
Bubcarrier.com.au

"Multitask (brush teeth with one hand, use other hand to clean sink.)"
Adrian Miller, Adrian Miller Sales Training
AdrianMiller.com

"No TV, no phone, no distractions; kids are either asleep or in school. Don't worry about chores or bills, just focus on the task at hand and you will exceed all your time management expectations."
Nitara Deratany, Deep Roots Consulting
DeepRootsConsulting.net

"Working at home with an infant, I've found that I can still be productive. I've gotten really good at working in strange positions: laying on my side with my arms draped over and around the baby; typing full e-mails with one hand; and even tooling around on my iPhone while I'm holding it over my reclined body. So take a deep breath, stretch, and work away! Just watch baby's hands when they reach for your keyboard or phone!"
Corrie Mieszczak, SoaringWinds Marketing
SoaringWindsMarketing.com

"There is no such thing as balance. Give up on the concept. Sometimes I am great at being a business owner, and sometimes I am great at being a mom. I am rarely great at both at the same time. Stop trying to multitask. Focus on what you are doing at the moment, and stop worrying about what you think you should be doing. You might be surprised to find that you are more efficient when you give something your full attention. Plus, you'll give yourself less grey hair!"
Cindy McCarthy, on the go Chicago
OnTheGoChicago.com

DONE 77. 78. 79 80. 81. 82. 83. 84. 85.

"To me, time management means divide and conquer. I separate business from family and only focus on one or the other at a time. When I'm working, work has my full attention and when I'm not, my family does."
Dawn Berryman, Market Mommy
MarketMommy.com

HIRE THEM

"Hire as many people as possible to help you! Nanny, sitter, grocery delivery service, housecleaner...it's worth giving up the date night for the sanity."
Genevieve Thiers
Sittercity.com

"Having a seriously strong support system is very important so that everyone helps each other with carpools, child care, whatever. It also helps to have a great backup plan as well—like keeping handy the number of your local errand runner."
Rhonna Costabile, Errands 911, Inc.
Errands911Inc.com

FIND TIME

"I find it helpful to get a handle on what lies ahead by checking my inbox and messages before the kids are awake. I might lose out on a couple of extra minutes of sleep by waking before my kids, but it gives me a sense of control over my hectic days and helps me prioritize within my limited work window."
Rebecca Rabson, SmartSeat Chair Protectors by pb&j Discoveries
SmartSeatDiningChairCovers.com

"I found that getting up an hour earlier to 'start' your day does actually help. Before the kids get up you can do your marketing for the day, return a couple of emails and return calls. Or the infamous

'Kitchen Counter Alarm' works too—if you finish your entry in fifteen minutes before the alarm goes off, it works every time."

Wendy Salazar, Stars Above Balloons Decor

Facebook.com/StarsAboveBalloons

"Something I find most useful is setting a time limit for tasks. For example, if you check your email several times a day, set a limit for how long you can check your email."

Pooja Gugnani, Organizing With You, Inc.

OrganizingWithYou.com

"Develop a daily discipline to set aside certain times of the day to accomplish certain things and stick with it. Behaviors, good or bad, eventually become habits, so be conscious of what patterns you are setting in your business."

Shira Adatto, Sheer Wellness

SheerWellness.net

COMPUTE THIS

"Close every window on your computer, silence your phone, set a timer and have a snack before starting any period of task accomplishment! No distractions maximizes the time you do have to get something completed."

Allison Cosmos, The Art & Design of Allison Cosmos

AllisonCosmos.com

"Download Freedom. It's a productivity application that locks down your Internet for as many hours as you need. Want to write that blog post? Shut it down for 45 minutes. Need to read that .pdf? Get the Internet out of your life and get some work done."

Roxy Weinstein, Hum With Us

STAY HEALTHY

"Get your pulse up. Get your blood flowing. SWEAT. There are two amazing things when you set aside an hour in your schedule for some exercise. First, this becomes YOUR time. If you're out on a run you can't be answering emails. But you can be thinking through in the back of your head what those emails can say. When you sit down to write them, they're already done. We may also think of our bodies and minds as separate, but if you let the body slack, the brain gets lazy too. Give your mind a body to live in that's not going to distract it. If you've got errands to run and you can bike or walk or jog there, do it. Remember, the time it takes to get to and from those errands is your hour of exercise. Turn off your phone and enjoy the trip. "

Alexis Finch, GraphiteMind

"Acknowledge that some days are just harder than others, and it's ok to start over. Sleep felt overrated until today when I set the teakettle to boil and realized I didn't refill the water... it was a sign to go back to bed. 22 minutes later, son #2 came in wanting breakfast. It was the most restful twenty-two minutes I've had in a very long time. We preach all the good things: eat well, sleep well, take time for yourself, your family and friends, balance... and then we go full steam ahead. Know when to wave the white flag and simple give yourself permission to rest."

Melissa, Grace Yoga And Pilates
Graceyoga-live-move-breathe.blogspot.com

"Don't forget to schedule your "you" time when planning your week. Have weekly pre-made snacks ready to grab on the go."

Jennifer Truesdale, STR8N UP Professional Organizing Services
Str8nup.org

GET OUT

"I find that I get more done when I work outside the home, so if I have a couple of hours between errands, I head to the coffee shop with my laptop to get things accomplished. If I try to work in my home office I'm often distracted by things like cleaning or laundry."
Paige Powell, Tub of Toys
TubofToys.com

THINK DIFFERENTLY

"Don't be afraid to grow slowly."
Bridget Juister L.Ac., B Holistic
BHolistic.com

"Don't waste time on things that didn't work out the way you thought they should. I remind myself that when speed bumps appear in the road that this challenge is not going to have an impact on my bigger picture. Then I move on and keep working towards the goal!"
Kirsty Mailer
KevinAndKirsty.com

"Have your vision clearly defined so that you know what to focus on each day. When life messes up your plan, reflect on your vision and moving toward it to get back on track and pick your next activity."
Emilie Shoop, Shoop Training & Consulting
Shooptc.com

"Though admirable,

you may want to take
"breastfeeding twins"
off your resume."

42 Heed Your Own Advice.

When writer Catherine Price asked Barry Glassner, Ph.D., sociologist, and author of *The Culture of Fear,* why we rely on guidebooks so much, "he hypothesized that it's because relying on experts alleviates our fear of the unknown and makes us feel more in control."

While this may be true, take most advice with a grain of salt. Particularly free advice. You get what you pay for. When "experts" are lecturing you, don't get sucked into their counsel, either. Even if they add "JD" or "CPA" to their title, they're not automatically go-to experts. *It's always an opinion.* It's so easy to get sucked in and take *this* attorney's well-intentioned advice, whose views are the complete opposite of *that* attorney's counsel because they have two different philosophies of the world. I myself have been swayed this way and that by different professionals discussing the pros and cons of forming an LLC and have been left completely confused about which way to turn. (And I went to *law school.*)

Educate yourself constantly, but steer clear of most website advice. Go ahead, roll your eyes. But you and I both know that when your kiddo has a cough or you feel a new back pain or you're worried about being sued, you Google it. And you scare the crap out of yourself. Stay informed and aware of what your friends are doing, what the news says, even what Steve Martin tweets (@SteveMartinToGo). But don't get sucked in. Everyone's view is just that: one view. **You ultimately need to gather information to form your own opinion and take your own advice.**

43 Stop Undervaluing Yourself.

If you take only one thing away from this book, take this: you are valuable. You have as much, if not more, to offer the world as an entrepreneur. So, stop undervaluing your services. Stop making super duper deals and bargains for customers on a regular basis. Stop offering constant discounts and breaks for clients. Just stop.

It's in our nature to be modest. We think that people will like us more if we act humble. And as women we constantly strive to be socially accepted, loved, and comforted. What's one way we accomplish this? To give and give and give—to our children, to our friends, to our neighbors, to total strangers.

But this is business. No one will like you more if you lower your rates. They will just think you're a chump. (You get what you pay for, right? That's what they're thinking, too). The more that you value yourself, the more you'll be recognized as being very valuable. In business, the general perception is that a higher price translates to higher quality. So get in there and play hardball—just don't price yourself outta the ballpark.

44 Take That Vacation.

The Center for Economic and Policy Research (CEPR) calls the United States the "No Vacation Nation," and for good reason. In a 2007 study, CEPR determined that "the U.S. is the only advanced economy in the world that doesn't guarantee paid vacation for employees."

What's up with that, employers?

We may take less vacation, but are we really more efficient than our European colleagues? The World Economic Forum shows that we remain the world's most competitive country. Yet other data, including countries' GDP per hours worked, reveal that Europe still gives America a run for its money. Many parts of the Old World are at least as productive as we are, if not more, with the added bonus of up to eight weeks off each year. And the average American gets a whopping 13 days to take a vacation. I think we Americans have something to learn.

If your business is up and running and you haven't left your corporate gig yet, it's probably time to go. Once you are your own boss and answer to no one but you, you can give yourself as much or as little time off as you so choose. Right? It's definitely one of the top ten reasons that entrepreneurs have given me as to why they left *the man* to work for themselves.

"OfficeMax®
isn't really a
toy store, is it?"

Excited about your new vacation schedule? Let me burst your entrepreneurial bubble. It just so happens that entrepreneurs, above all other Americans, take even *less* time off for vacation than the average employee of a major corporation. Yep, you heard me: less. Entrepreneurs usually won't pay themselves a livable salary in the early years and will often forgo real vacations until their business is financially sound. That can often take eight years or longer, says William Bygrave, a professor emeritus of entrepreneurship at Babson College in Wellesley, Massachusetts. Perhaps it's the desire to prove oneself, or perhaps it's the reality that the onus rests entirely on the entrepreneur to make some dough. Either way, it happens. Is this pressure really necessary? Is your goal to work yourself to the bone while raising your children so that you're overworked, underpaid, and unhealthy? I didn't think so.

Let's think this through. When do you make your best decision? *When you're on the potty, correct?* When does that genius idea hit you so hard that you could fall over? *When you're taking a shower, no?* When are you most productive? *When you're working out, right?* Take time to clear your head. Take advantage of being your own boss. If it takes getting an intern, skipping a networking event, taking on one less project, or hiring a new employee—do it. Take a vacation. Don't have enough money saved up? Take a staycation. That counts, too. Return as a person who is more efficient, more creative, and more productive. The time you take off now will save you a ton of time in the long run.

45 Play More Music.

Turn that iPod on. Blast your car stereo. Pump up your Pandora tunes. Since music improves brain function you might as well listen to more of it. I can't concentrate on *anything*, including hearing myself think, unless there's music on while I'm working. Check out what happens to your body, literally, if you turn on your favorite music after a long day. It doesn't have to be Mozart or an opera. Get loose with Rush or Lady Gaga, The Beatles or Nicki Minaj, Van Halen or

Adele—whoever floats your boat. The sensory experience of a great melody, great lyrics, or a simple beat can totally make your mood swing in the right direction.

You know those days where you wake up in the morning, read your emails, and all of them make you angry? You were ready for a great day, right? Why do people have to be so mean and ruin it? You're about to hit reply and begin a barrage of not-so-nice responses when your pre-schooler walks into your office. She demands that you put an Amy Winehouse song on for the 423rd time. In order to control yourself from getting even more upset, you're about to write your child a "WTF?" email that she can read in 20 years, but realizing it will take less time to watch the darn thing, you oblige and open a YouTube video of Ms. Winehouse telling your three-year old that she will not go to rehab. And then…by the end of the first verse, your shoulders relax. You get up out of your chair and have a two-minute dance party with her. By the song's end, you kick her out of your office, sit back down and re-read your morning emails. You'll be darned if you can't remember why you were so angry before.

Incorporate music into your daily routine. If you don't remember to turn music on more often, maybe this is a job that you can give to your kids.

46 Prep Dinner in the Morning.

When you wake up, you can barely stomach breakfast and already you're expected to bring out the dinner ingredients? I know it's counterintuitive, but believe me, it's incredibly helpful.

If you want to get it all done, get more organized about it. Collect all your recipes on the weekend and buy the appropriate groceries. Spend 30 minutes every morning prepping that night's meal. Pre-chop the veggies. Put the spices and condiments on the counter. Make sure you aren't missing any ingredients. That way, when you look up at your computer's clock and it says 5 pm, you don't have to experience the Daily Freakout: How am I going to cook dinner? What are we going to eat? Where are the takeout menus?

Once you have that routine down, one-up yourself by heading to RelishRelish.com. They're the best concoction since sliced bread. They offer a new menu each week. Pick your recipes and the site will not only aggregate your shopping list for you, but it will also make sure that meals take under 30 minutes to prep and are under $90 in total grocery bills—and that's for five entrees and sides. They have a stringent meal testing program and proactively interact with customers about likes, dislikes, and what might possibly be the best Super Moist Chocolate Cake that anyone's ever tasted. You can also head to DreamDinners.com. This site enables you to select any combination of that month's selected dinners, sides, or desserts (a minimum of 36 servings per order), show up to one of their locations to assemble the dishes with other participants, and then head home to either cook those meals up or store them in your freezer for future use. You can even grab some friends and have a private 'meal assembly' party at one of their kitchens. And then there's TheFresh20.com. Save money, save time and get healthy by picking 20 fresh ingredients to make 5 budget-friendly dinners each week. What could be easier?

These sites are lifesavers, I tell you.

4 INGREDIENTS ✚ NO KNEADING =
FRESH BREAD

- 3 cups lukewarm water
- 1.5 packets granulated yeast
- 1.5 T salt
- 6.5 cups all-purpose white flour

Add the yeast and salt to the water in a mixing bowl. Mix in the flour. No need to knead! You are welcome to use a food processor if you are as addicted to kitchen gadgets as I am. Really, don't knead. **Return three phone calls instead.**

Cover the bowl with a lid but don't make it airtight or you'll be sorry about the ensuing explosion in the kitchen. Let it rise for 2 hours, up to 5 hours if you have to tend to carpool. You can refrigerate it overnight "for better results" **(i.e. for more e-mailing time).**

Sprinkle water on top and then shape it into two loose balls in 30-60 seconds on a cookie sheet. Add a little flour if too sticky. Let it sit on the counter for an hour and **clean your desk up a bit, will you?**

Preheat oven to 450. Dust the tops with flour and bake for about 30 minutes until the crusts are brown.

It's delish! And it fed my family for two days straight.

47 Stay Focused.

The other day, I met with an old male colleague who told me about someone that I should meet. She and I would get along well, he said, but she's just so *different* from me. Why? Because she's "Because she's focused," he said. OK, so where's the different part? It took me a few minutes to realize what he was saying, because I never thought about myself as anything but focused.

The fact that I've started three companies doesn't seem to make sense to nontrepreneurial folks. To them, we might look scattered, flaky, unfocused, or downright lazy. Don't bother arguing with them about it. It's not going to work. You can't convince the traditional-ists that what you have is special. You're a creative well of ideas and these ideas spring up when you least expect it. It's what makes you an entrepreneur. The ability to come up with an idea and follow through? Check. The sense to take what was just a neuron firing in your brain and turn it into a profitable company? Check. The where-withal to finish what you start, even if it happens to be five different things that you start al the same time? Pure genius.

"Unfocused" is the layman's way of saying, "I couldn't possibly understand what you are doing, or how you do it." Don't even bother. Waste of energy. You are awesome.

48 Shrug it Off.

In kindergarten, I had a hard time understanding why people didn't like each other. What's not to like? I'm nice, you're nice. Of course we'll get along. I even misunderstood the word "children" and thought that if I was Jill, all of my friends were "Jilldren."

That was then, and this is now. Once you launch your business, consider yourself under attack. At all times. Let's start with notes and calls from unhappy customers. Dissatisfied clients are always fun. And those suddenly-broke, nonpaying customers are just the best. It can get even worse if you comment on a popular blog and people aim their fire at your character, never mind your comment.

Des Moines, Iowa's safer but no-less-festive:

RUNNING OF THE MOMS

If you land an incredible PR opportunity, maybe an appearance on Good Morning America or a product feature in a national magazine, there's hate aplenty to go around. Ignore and move along.

My sister-in-law called me one day and said,

"Go to PerezHilton.com right now. Right now."

I clicked, and there in all her glory was Gwen Stefani holding her baby Zuma who was wearing **MY PRODUCT!!!!!!!** (note appropriate usage of exclamation points here.) My heart stopped. I told my computer to "get outta here" three hundred times. And then with a tweak of my finger and a slight scroll of the page, I saw all of the Debbie Downers of the world unite on this website. "Why would anyone buy this product and put it on their baby?" said one commenter. "The person selling these must be crazy!" Had I paid attention to those posts, I'd have given up and gone out of business a long time ago. But I got over it. I learned to shrug it off, and here I am.

Focus on the good stuff. Ignore morons and Debbie Downers. Client feedback about your product or service is important, whether positive or negative, since it is really a guide to help your business grow, improve, and succeed. But anonymous blog comments? Scathing reviews by people that post under the alias FuzzyNinjaBanana? Let it go. Anonymity tends to put people in attack mode, so these comments may not be the most reliable place to get feedback. Stay away from anonymous criticism and stay focused on the opinions and comments that really matter.

49 Get Inspired.

Seth Godin, marketing genius and prolific thinker on all things business, had this to say about starting a company:
"**Lesson 1:** In fact, you can make a difference, you can start something from scratch, you can build something without authority or permission. Passionate people on a mission can make change happen. **Lesson 2:** In fact, philanthropy works. Building systems and enhancing entrepreneurial outcomes generates results far bigger than the resources invested. **Lesson 3:** You better be prepared to stick it out, to exert yourself, to last longer than you ever expected and to care so much it hurts."

Seth brought this up in relation to the 10th anniversary of the Acumen Fund, an organization dedicated to creating a world beyond poverty (as per their website.) They think big, don't they? Because of Acumen, more than 3 million people have access to safe, affordable, and efficient energy. Seven thousand people have jobs. Hundreds of millions of insecticide-treated bed nets have been provided. All thanks to a "small band of talented, driven people."

There are inspiring stories like this one everywhere. You just have to know where to look. Instead of seeking out competition and trying to find stories of failed entrepreneurs to make you feel better about what you're doing, you can choose to seek out successful organizations that are thriving. Read publications like Inc. Magazine and Fast Company Magazine or watch TED Talks at TED.com to get inspired by great companies. Examine the types of people who make up these organizations. Look at how their founders conduct business in the world. And if you can start small, like Acumen did, you can inch toward a greater good in whatever you are doing. Patience is a virtue when it comes to using your entrepreneurship to make a difference in the world, big or small.

GET A PEN

"_____!" she screamed.
(Exclamation)

"What, am I supposed to get paid in _____?"
(noun)
She didn't want to be near her

_____ anymore, didn't want to check
(noun)

_____ or _____ again,
(name of social media site)   (name of social media site)
and stormed off to the _____ to cook
(room of house)
dinner. She whipped out the

_____ and started chopping the
(kitchen utensil)

_____ to make a salad. But in a fit of
(vegetable)

_____, she forgot that she shouldn't touch
(mood)

her _____ after chopping it up. And her
(body part)

_____ did get itchy indeed. So she
(body part)

scratched it. And the _____ sensation that
(feeling)

crawled up from her _____ to her
(body part)

_____ made her feel so outrageously
(body part)

_____ that she gave up. Bottle of _____
(adjective)   (alcohol)

in hand, she ate _____ _____ and
(big number)   (favorite candy)

ordered takeout.

50 Ignorance is Bliss.
This is not your ordinary love story.

A girl walks into a bar. She approaches a boy in thick glasses. He looks at her quizzically. She introduces herself. Throughout her five-minute pitch, he stays quiet. He's entranced by her words and he nods periodically at her animated face. She finishes. He gives her a smile. They shake hands, and she leaves. She's quite proud of herself, and a wee bit excited.

It took me years to realize that the boy in the bar actually thought that I was an incompetent amateur. He was being nice, and I will always be grateful for his kindness.

I had just started my music management firm, Paperwork Media. I wanted to book my artists to play shows in venues all over the country. What occurred to me as a great first step? Call each venue and make an appointment with the talent buyer (the gal or guy who books bands there) so that I could introduce myself in person. Which I did more than several times.

I eventually booked local bands and internationally-renowned artists to play venues around the world. I learned the ins and outs of booking, effective ways of doing so, and the do's and don'ts of the industry. What's number one on that list of don'ts? It's written on most venues' websites in their "booking policy" section: *"1. Don't walk in, drop off CDs, or even call us. If we dig the music we hear online, we will contact you."* Oops.

I was clearly in the wrong, but apparently so inept at my job that these talent buyers took pity on me. I was the epitome of an amateur. If I were to recount the amount of mistakes that I've made like this one, it would take up twelve tomes. But had I not made them, I would not be here. It behooves you and your business to get out there, screw up often, and learn. If you're scared to be wrong, figure out how to get out of the wonderful world of entrepreneurship fast.

Now, go make some mistakes.

RESOURCES

What would we do without the internet?

The sites listed here are mentioned in the book along with a few extras for good measure.

Know of more helpful resources than those listed here?

Head to FoundingMoms.com/Forum and please post them in our Resources forum.

Seek and ye shall find it.

RESOURCES

FIND THE FOUNDING MOMS
FoundingMoms.com/Forum
Facebook.com/FoundingMoms
FoundingMoms.com/GamePlan
FoundingMoms.com
FoundingMoms.com/Member-Directory
LinkedIn.com/in/foundingmom
Twitter.com/FoundingMom (or @FoundingMom)

ACCOUNTING
Freshbooks.com
InDinero.com
LessAccounting.com
Mint.com
Peachtree.com
Quickbooks.com
Quicken.com

BARTER
Bitly.com/jillclip (The Man Who Traded A Red Paperclip For A House)
NeighborGoods.net
U-Exchange.com

COMMUNICATION
FreeConferenceCalls.com
FuzeMeeting.com
GoToMeeting.com
UStream.com
Skype.com
Vokle.com

COOKING

DreamDinners.com
RelishRelish.com
TheFresh20.com

CROWDSOURCING

Crowdspring.com
Kickstarter.com
Prosper.com

DOMAIN NAMES

Domain Name Generator:
http://www.selfseo.com/domain_typo_generator.php
GoDaddy.com
Namecheap.com

EDUCATIONAL SITES

E-How.com
Mashable.com
Squidoo.com

HOSTING

GoDaddy.com
PhillipsData.com

INSPIRATION

bitly.com/jillsted (my TED talk!)
FastCompany.com
Inc.com
Ted.com

RESOURCES

LEGAL
AdamSalzman.com
Bit.ly/feinapp (Federal Employment ID Number)
IncSmart.biz (Incorporation Helpers)
LegalZoom.com

MISCELLANEOUS AWESOME SITES
ArtisanalPencilSharpening.com
Evisors.com
IdeaPaint.com
Micromentor.com
Pinterest.com
WorkingMomsAgainstGuilt.com

NETWORK
FoundingMoms.com/Forum
FoundingMoms.com/Meetups
SBA.gov

SOCIAL MEDIA
Facebook.com
Foursquare.com
Hootsuite.com
Knowem.com
LinkedIn.com
Tweetdeck.com
Twitter.com

START A BLOG
Blogger.com
Tumblr.com
Wordpress.com

SURVEY SITES
Docs.Google.com
SurveyMonkey.com
Wufoo.com

TOOLS
FoundingMoms.com/GamePlan
NeighborGoods.net
Tadalist.com

VIRTUAL ASSISTANCE
Craigslist.org
FancyHands.com
ivaa.org
oDesk.com
TasksEveryDay.com

JOHN HARTZELL, ILLUSTRATIONS

John Hartzell is a joke writer and an electrical engineer with Underwriters Laboratories, where he performs safety assessments of commercial cooking equipment. You're welcome.

John has created two comic strips using the same clipart-with-captions formula: Cliptoons and Middle Age Riot. The former set the Internet abuzz for several seconds before dying a death in the early part of this century. The latter continues to educate and enlighten - edulighten, if you will - from its website at MiddleAgeRiot.com and on Facebook.

John lives with his lovely wife and two lovely children (and slightly-less-lovely cat and downright ugly dog) in the domestic bliss of an unnamed western suburb of Chicago (hint: it's Oak Park.) In his free time John fidgets nervously, wondering what the hell he's supposed to be doing. And he likes drive-ins.